A PORTRAIT OF
GREECE

Terri Hardin

TODTRI

This book was designed and produced by
TODTRI Book Publishers
254 West 31st Street
New York, NY 10001-2813
Fax: (212) 695-6984
E-mail: info@todtri.com

Visit us on the web!
www.todtri.com

Printed and bound in Korea

ISBN 1-57717-088-1

Author: Terri Hardin

Publisher: Robert M. Tod
Editors: Mary Forsell, Joanna Wissinger, Don Kennision
Designer: Mark Weinberg
Production Co-ordinator: Heather Weigel
DTP Associate: Adam Yellin
Typesetting: Command-O Design

PHOTO CREDITS

Photographer/Page Number

Mike Barlow/Dembinsky Photo Associates 101

Randa Bishop 6, 7, 22, 30 (bottom), 95, 97 (top), 97 (bottom), 99, 118,120-121, 124, 128 (top),128 (bottom), 129, 130 (top)

Charles Bowman 5, 8-9, 10, 36, 50 (top), 52, 53, 59, 69, 83, 84, 85, 119, 122, 127, 135, 139 (bottom), 142, 143

Jean S. Buldain 11, 46, 62, 63 (top), 67, 68 (top, right), 68 (bottom), 96, 100 (bottom)

Ron Chapple/FPG International 17 (bottom)

Gill S.J. Copeland/Nawrocki Stock Photo 33, 55

Byron Crader/Ric Ergenbright Photography 21, 27 (top), 45, 66, 68 (top, left), 102 (left), 114

Bill Holden 123, 126, 132, 133, 141 (top)

Doranne Jacobson 17 (top)

Jeff Louis 27 (bottom), 98, 100 (top, left), 100 (top, right), 102 (right), 103 (top), 106, 107, 108 (top), 110-111

G. Marche/FPG International 49

Buddy Mays/Travel Stock 16 (top), 18-19, 26, 38, 39, 40-41, 42, 44, 47, 50 (bottom), 51, 63 (bottom), 64, 65, 77, 136-137, 138, 139 (top), 141 (bottom)

W. S. Nawrocki 30 (top), 134

Eberhard E. Otto/FPG International 56-57, 58 (bottom), 82, 125

Vladimir Pcholkin/FPG International 48

Robert Fried Photography 13, 16 (bottom), 24-25, 28, 29, 31, 35 (top), 35 (bottom), 58 (top), 70, 71, 72-73, 74 (left), 74 (right), 75, 76, 78 (top), 78 (bottom), 79, 80, 81 (top), 81 (bottom), 86, 87, 88-89, 90 (top), 90 (bottom), 91 (top), 91 (bottom), 92 (top), 92 (bottom), 93, 104-105, 108 (bottom), 109, 112, 113, 116 (top), 116 (bottom), 117, 140

Charles E. Schmidt 32, 34

Charles Schabes/Nawrocki Stock Photo 60, 61 (top), 61 (bottom)

Timmerman Foto-Presse/Nawrocki Stock Photo 23

Steve Vidler/Nawrocki Stock Photo 14, 15, 20, 43, 54, 94, 115, 130 (bottom), 131

Richard Walker/Nawrocki Stock Photo 37

Toyohiro Yamada/FPG International 103 (bottom)

TABLE OF CONTENTS

Fishing remains one of the principal industries of Greece. In the town of Nea Mondamia on the peninsula of Halkidiki, fishermen prepare their nets.

Introduction

Greece, a country that borders both Europe and the Near East, a country that is mostly mountains, sun-baked plains, and scattered islands, is nevertheless greatly responsible for the course of Western civilisation. Songs first sung in 850 BC inspire us today and concepts of government first proposed in the fifth century BC provide modern democracies with their basic structure. Even the word 'democracy', meaning 'government by the people', is Greek: it describes the Athenian system by which all citizens—from aristocrats to farmers—had say in their government.

Although Greek history will be explored further in other chapters, it is essential first to outline the sequence of events that explains the significance of Greece in the history of western Europe. Here then is a short introduction to Greece and its past.

Although Greece, like the rest of Europe, had civilised settlements in one form or another since Neolithic times, the most important one, which since has had a great influence on Western thought and tradition, began in Athens around the fifth century BC. Athens, a city-state whose Olympian patron was Athena, the goddess of wisdom, had devised a system in which all men participated and had an active say in how the 'polis' (city) was governed. The Athenian assembly was composed of all male citizens, who assembled at specific times to discuss the issues before them, and together they voted on how to proceed. Thus, the assembly was the first practising democracy.

Ostracism was a common way of ensuring that leaders of the Assembly did not get too powerful. Taken from the Greek word 'ostrakos' (meaning potsherd), it signifies the method by which exiles were selected. Those who wished to exile an offender wrote his name on a piece of broken pottery which was cast into a vessel. An ostracised citizen was exiled from Athens for a period of five to ten years.

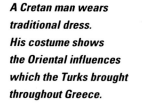

Classical Athens prospered under its leader Pericles. It was a time of expansion that saw the construction of many important buildings, among them the Parthenon and the Erectheum atop the Acropolis, and the Temple of Poseidon at Cape Sounion on the eastern end of the Attic peninsula. Athens's fleet enjoyed supremacy of the sea and Athenian culture was at its zenith, but all was soon to fade. From 431 to 404 BC, the Peloponnesian Wars weakened Athens's hold on the sea and its culture began to decline.

In the end, the democratic constitution, so long cherished by Athens, was suspended, and the city fell into the hands of the repressive Spartans. One significant aspect of their degeneration was the death of Socrates, forced to drink hemlock as an enemy of the state. His student, the philosopher Plato, immortalised his passing and other encounters in his famous work, the Dialogues.

After the fall of Athens, there followed years of fighting between the Greek city-states and the Persian Empire, in alliances which formed and collapsed with equal rapidity. Then, in 336 BC, Alexander of Macedon began his thirteen-year conquest of the known world. Although the Macedonians were considered barbarians by Athenian standards, they had for generations been ardent admirers of Greek culture. Alexander adopted the art and the philosophy of Athens, and in his conquering sweep of the ancient world from Greece to India, planted the seeds of its culture everywhere.

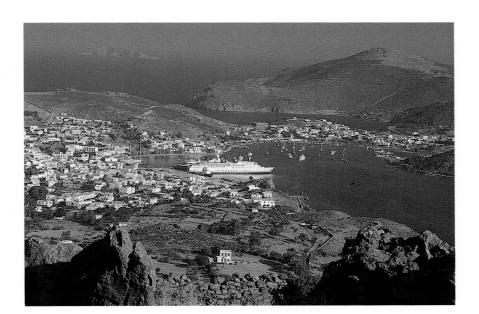

His attitude of 'Greek is best' was hardly shared by the conquered. Indeed, many of the Greek rulers which he put into place as his proxies were not only virtually isolated in the societies they closed to 'foreigners', but with the death of Alexander they were cut off from contact with Greece and gradually adopted the customs of the place they ruled. When Alexander died in 323 BC, the Macedonian Empire collapsed. Within a century, it was part of the Roman Empire.

The Romans were just as rapacious as Alexander in their appetite for empire, and just as convinced of their superior culture, but they also recognised the Greeks' accomplishments in arts, philosophy, and the sciences, and they imported them wholesale.

Still, the Romans had a contrary attitude towards the Greeks. Though their children were tutored by Greeks and the teachings of Greek philosophy were widely known, and though the Greek dialect, 'koine', was more common throughout the Empire than Latin— still the Romans would not acknowledge the achievements they owed to the Greeks. It was as if they were ashamed to be beholden to a captive people.

Like Alexander, the Romans were great builders. Thus, Roman ruins are often to be found among those of earlier times throughout Greece, and often they are in better condition. For example, little remains of what was ancient Corinth, which the Romans sacked and occupied in the first century AD, apart from those ruins dating from Roman times.

With the decline of the Roman Empire came events that would once again reshape the face of Europe. Menaced by Germanic invaders, the city of Rome was no longer a safe place to be. In 324, the Emperor Constantine moved the centre of the Roman Empire to Constantinople, in Turkey (now Istanbul). In 313, he had made an even more significant move: he made Christianity a legal religion.

Christianity, the religion out of the Middle East, had been steadily gaining converts since its introduction. Greece and Asia Minor were visited by the evangelical Paul and others; Saint Luke, one of the authors of the New Testament, was himself a Greek, and Saint John had been exiled to the Greek isle of Patmos. By becoming a Christian himself,

Skala harbour, near the town of Chora on the island of Patmos, is a perfect Mediterranean berth: small, but deep enough for larger craft. Whitewashed buildings line the harbour.

Following page: Athens, whose timelessness is symbolised by the Acropolis, was actually lost to time for many centuries. Languishing from the Byzantine era onwards, it once again came into its own as the capital of Greece in the nineteenth century.

Constantine led the way for it to become the state religion, thus founding what would later become the Holy Roman Empire.

Voltaire, the French philosopher of the Enlightenment, once mused that the Holy Roman Empire was 'neither holy, nor Roman, nor was it an empire'. One could argue that it was indeed an empire, though it is probably unnecessary to argue its holiness. But as for Roman? It was more Greek than anything.

Like Alexander's ruling Greeks, the Roman ruling class had set itself up amidst a world of strangers; it was only a matter of time before it was assimilated by those it had conquered. By Constantine's time, koine, which had been the trade language throughout the ancient world, was the language of the Church as well.

It is important to realise that throughout history Greek civilisation encompassed not only the homeland but the entire Aegean coast. Homer first sang his epics on the coasts of Asia Minor, and Schliemann discovered Troy in Turkey. The lyric poetry of Sappho and Alcaeus is distinguished by the soft Aegan S 'melissa' instead of the hard Attic T 'melitta'. And so even though Athens was diminished, the Greek world was thriving. When, in the sixth century, the Greek woman Theodora became the wife of the Emperor, Justinian the Great, the glory that was Greece had again come into its own.

Like its Roman Catholic counterpart in Europe, the Greek Orthodox church was gaining in influence. Of lasting importance to the modern world has been its preservation of the physical relics of early Christianity. Although generally underappreciated in the West, Orthodoxy has consistently safeguarded the Christian faith in the wake of many serious obstacles, including Ottoman rule and the contemporary predations of Communism. Monasteries founded at the dawn of Christianity have sustained some of the greatest artifacts of the Christian past.

Many significant religious disagreements sundered the Roman Catholic church from the Greek Orthodox, but power and the right to self-determination had much to do with it as well. They united briefly in the fifteenth century, but soon again parted company.

The Byzantine Empire also faced challenges from barbarians. The term 'barbarian' remained in use, although some of them were now Roman Catholics. The Peloponnesos, for example, was conquered by the Slavic Avars in about 590, and held

Monastics are fond of inaccessible places, as the Monastery of St Nicholas attests. It is set in the midst of the Porto Lago harbour, on Lake Vistonis in Thrace.

as theirs for centuries afterward. From this time on, the Byzantine emperors maintained only a tenuous hold on their claim of empire.

In 867, a Macedonian named Basil I was proclaimed emperor of Byzantium, beginning a dynasty that lasted for almost two centuries, stemming the barbarian tide and granting some stability to the fragile empire. His namesake, Basil II, was also called 'the Bulgar-Slayer'; he defeated the Bulgarians in 1014. With his reign began a renaissance of Byzantine art, culminating with the Sancta Sophia in Thessaloniki, the monasteries at Dafni, Mount Athos, and the Meteora in Thessaly.

It was the Crusaders, seeking to liberate the Holy Land, who finally broke up the Byzantine Empire. First appearing as pilgrims in the tenth century, they took to plundering in the twelfth, looting the great cities of Corfu, Thessaloniki (then Salonika), and Constantinople.

The Venetians were also an imperial power, especially in the islands. From the thirteenth century on, and almost every island in the Ionian and Aegean Seas, both important and not so important, boasts a Venetian fortress. In fact, the Venetian hold upon the islands and the Peloponnesos was so great that it was maintained until the eighteenth century.

Vergina was, at one time, the centre of the Macedonian empire. These ruins are of a Hellenistic palace, built in the third century BC after Alexander, and comprise only part of the wonders found in this historic area.

Near last in this succession of occupiers come the Turks, but they, like the Venetians, were tenacious, holding onto the Greek mainland from the fifteenth century to the eighteenth, and eventually wresting some islands away from the Venetians and other Europeans.

Under the Ottoman Empire, the Greeks were taxed twice as much (as were all of its subject peoples) as the dominating Turks. Nonetheless, some considered this better than being under Venetian rule, where taxes were even heavier. Also, under the Turks the Greeks were granted complete religious freedom, and a certain amount of self-rule under the Orthodox Patriarch; in their Greek duchies, the Venetians preferred to rule. Still, by the early nineteenth century, many Greeks—encouraged by European countries such as England and France—began to envision the possibility of revolt against the Turks, followed by self-rule.

The Greek War of Independence began in 1821 and culminated in independence in 1832. Having helped the Greeks achieve self-government, the Europeans then selected a king to rule them. While their first choice, Prince Otto of Bavaria, was deposed, the second, Prince William of Denmark, ruled as King George I and helped to bring about much-needed reforms.

In both World Wars, Greece was on the side of the Allies, although it was occupied by both Italy and Germany. During World War II, Greece was liberated with the help of the British, but civil war immediately erupted, and blood was shed in Athens's central Syntagma Square. The civil war was resolved in 1949, and the King, who had been out of the country since the beginning of World War II, returned and placed a wreath on the Tomb of the Unknown Soldier in front of the Royal Palace.

Greece again erupted in civil strife in the early 1960s when a military junta brought the government to a standstill and forced King Constantine to flee. The junta, which was right-wing in nature and sought to block the liberal victory of Andreas Papandreou, lasted from 1967 to 1974. The colonels' symbol—one which became much despised—was the phoenix.

The socialist PASOK party of Papandreou was founded in 1974, just at the end of the colonels' junta; it came to power in 1981. Since then, Greece has tried to adjust to the modern European community, joined the Common Market, and opened itself up to widespread tourism.

As it has done so often in the past, the world has responded by flocking to the timeless world of Greece, to view the ruins of history gone by, and to bask on the miles of beaches in the pure, brilliant sunlight.

What follows are descriptions of some of Greece's most noted sights and most visited islands—both of which are too numerous to contain fully within these covers.

The Monastery of St Nicholas Anapafsas is part of the Meteoran complex; it was founded in the fourteenth century.

Athens

Athens, the birthplace of democracy and modern drama, epitomises for many the best of all things Greek. It is one of the oldest cities in the world, having been inhabited continuously for almost three thousand years. But in spite of its history, Athens is in every way a modern city; and perhaps this, too, is the legacy of Classical times, when fifth-century BC Athenians were noted for their love of novelty.

Nowadays, though contemporary areas such as Omonia Square show the signs of systematic planning, there are also places where old and new exist side by side, sometimes in surprising ways, as when Hadrian's Arch rises up from the edge of a busy multilane highway.

The Parthenon, that eternal symbol of ancient Greece, is visible from most parts of the city, standing high upon the Acropolis (*acropolis* means 'high city', and there are many to be seen in towns throughout Greece). It is an impressive sight, still standing in spite of thousands of years of foreign predations, not to mention the decades of caustic air pollution that have been eating steadily away at it and other antiquities; under these circumstances, it sometimes seems remarkable that anything remains. It has seen conquerors of all kinds, some of whom have carted away large chunks of it. The British Museum and the Louvre are among the offenders, and the Greeks have long agitated for the return of their treasures.

Possession of Greek archaeological antiquities—foreign or private, lawful or otherwise—is now a bitter bone of contention. The Greeks resent having to make due with inferior replicas. The trade in

This is the view which first presents itself to visitors as they pass through the Acropolis admission gate. The Parthenon, which can be seen from practically any point in the city, is even more imposing at close range.

antiquities, which enjoyed huge popularity during the 1980s, is slowly trickling to a halt. The results are clear in the auction room: Sotheby's was recently unable to auction off a Cycladic sculpture. However, the government of Greece is also generous with museum loans, so the rest of the world is able to enjoy Greek antiquities on a regular, legal basis.

The Acropolis is a hot, steady climb from the city below, but it is possible to rest and find refreshment on the way. On the day of our arrival, it was closed for a half-hour strike—a show of strength on the part of the unions. We sat down on the sandy, splintery rocks near the admission booth, with the hot sun beating on our heads, and waited.

There was a marvelous view of the city. Looking down from the Acropolis on high, much of Athens seems lost in time. From our vantage point, we saw some of the older parts of the city which are close by: the Plaka, a neighbourhood of old houses; the Monastiraki district, whose famous flea market is a striking feature of the former

At night, coloured lights directed on the Parthenon produce a dramatic effect that can be seen throughout the city. Visitors as well as citizens are invited to contemplate this enduring symbol of the city's history.

The buildings upon the Acropolis became—as they were meant to be— the crowning achievement of Pericles' Athens. The architect Ictinus designed the Parthenon, while the famed sculptor Phidias oversaw its construction and created the statue of Athena.

Six sculptures of maidens (caryatids) uphold the porch attached to the Erectheum. Although dramatic in their setting, these are only plaster replicas; the real thing can be seen in the British Museum and in the Museum of the Acropolis nearby.

In 1896, the Olympic Games were reestablished, this time in Athens. The Greeks, understandably sentimental about their contribution to the history of sports and peace, were dismayed when the American city of Atlanta, Georgia, was chosen to host the games on its centenary.

The Theatre of Dionysus, a structure dating from the Classical period, can be found near the Plaka. It is the historic site where the plays of the great tragedians—Aeschylus, Sophocles, and Euripides—and the comedian Aristophanes were first heard and judged by the Athenian populace.

Turkish quarter; and newer structures in the distance. After a short while, the strike was over, the admission booth opened, and we were allowed to enter the Acropolis's eternal precincts.

Close by the entrance, an old photographer with an ancient camera took black-and-white photographs of couples posing in front of the Parthenon. Judging by his samples, he had been doing this since the end of World War II, at least. He developed his pictures (which seemed almost as timeless as their backdrop) in a bucket of water, on which pigeons alight and drink.

The Parthenon was the glory of Periclean Athens; some of the most famous artists of antiquity shared in its creation. It was built under the supervision of the sculptor Phidias (who created the statue of Athena) and Ictinus, its primary architect, assisted by Callicrates. Its stone, a yellowish marble, was quarried at nearby Mount Pentelicon.

It was completed between 447 and 432 BC. The outer walls had *metopes* (carved plaques that form part of the frieze) numbering ninety-two, the inner walls a frieze showing the procession of Athena; the centre of which was the presentation of the *peplos*, or 'robe', of Athena, placed on the shoulders of her statue during the festival of the Panathenaia, which occurred every four years. A triangular

The Temple of Zeus was begun by Pissistratos in 515 BC, but completed by the Emperor Hadrian in AD 132. Monumental even by ancient standards, it is considered to be the largest temple dedicated to Zeus in Greece.

The Museum of Athens is built in the Neoclassic mode in order to blend harmoniously with its collections. This long, covered arcade—called a stoa—*is one of the features of Classical design. It lent its name to the philosophers (Stoics) who used to teach from its steps.*

Syntagma, or Constitution, Square, is the lively centre of modern-day Athens. Cafes, luxury hotels and shops, and the Royal Palace border the square, while the Plaka is a short walk away.

pediment on the east side showed the birth of Athena, and on the west, the contest of Athena and Poseidon for Athens.

Also atop the Acropolis is the Erectheum, with the famous Porch of the Maidens (also known as *caryatids*) attached to it on the left. It was completed soon after the Parthenon. When it became a Christian church a thousand years later (in the fifth century AD), many of its treasures were removed or defaced. The most significant destruction, however, occurred in 1687, when the occupying Turks used the temple as an arsenal and the Venetians fired upon it, causing some of the stored ammunition to explode. Further destruction was accomplished by European explorers and treasure hunters such as Lord Elgin, who hauled off priceless antiquities to the British Museum.

The maidens now in place are plaster replicas, however; those caryatids (named after the priestesses of Artemis in Caryae, Laconia, in the Peleponnesos) which have remained in Greece are now housed in the Acropolis Museum, along with many other of the more fragile items, including some fragments of the Parthenon frieze, and several statues, including some sixth-century figures and the famous Victory undoing her sandal.

The Parthenon and the surrounding buildings have undergone extensive restoration in the past hundred years, some as late as the 1980s. To many, the ruins atop the Acropolis epitomise the Classical world and its restraint from the hurly-burly of colour and caricature, but it is not really a true vision of that age. After all, what are seen today as ruins were new and vividly alive in the age of Pericles; what is now bleached by sun, climate, and passage of time was once brilliantly coloured. In fact, the Classical times of Pericles were anything but restrained; they saw both the flowering of democracy and imperialist expansion, the flourishing of the arts, and the eventual defeat of all they sought to achieve.

Modernity has not been kind to the ancient world; earthquakes have rocked the Parthenon, and air pollution from car exhaust has eaten away at the Greeks' treasured antiquity. About a third of Greece's population—roughly four million—lives in Athens, but this fraction owns three-quarters of all motor vehicles. In recent years, the Greeks have attempted to ease the situation by passing environmental laws, such as

The new Olympic arena was built in Athens in 1896 to celebrate the revival of the ancient rites. The modern-day games have only been interrupted by World Wars I and II.

Following page:
In Classical times, Athens' port Piraeus saw the launching of the great Athenian fleet. Nowadays, its industry is maintained by tourists eager to get to the sunny islands.

The National Archaeological Museum displays items discovered in Greece's two thousand archaeological sites, such as this ancient ceramic vase, decorated with patterns of leaves.

banning cars in Athens and creating incentives for the use of lower-emission vehicles elsewhere. But it is not only antiquities which feel the sting of nature. Because of earthquakes and tremors in Athens, many modern, steel-framed buildings are no more than a dozen floors high.

From atop the Acropolis one can look out in any direction. One can see, for example, the Areopagus, the ancient seat of judgement. Orestes is said to have sought expiation there, and Saint Paul is said to have mounted its steps in order to preach the gospel.

Returning to central Syntagma Square, my travelling partners and I witnessed the changing of the sentries in front of the former Palace (now the Parliament Building) and the Tomb of the Unknown Soldier. It is fitting that this monument should stand here, since fierce fighting and carnage filled the Square during the Civil and Second World Wars. The sentries (called *evzones*) are dressed in magnificent uniforms of oriental splendour, ending in heavy white stockings and shoes with large pom-poms. The evzones are objects of wonder, from tourists taking snapshots to young scamps and flirtatious girls (who try to make the guards break their concentration). The changing of the sentries occurs every hour; and on Sundays, units of evzones parade.

Behind the Parliament, the National Garden is a place to get away from the bustle of tourists and traffic along the Ermou, a broad, straight boulevard. Quiet tree-lined avenues and out-of-the-way nooks abound, and it is possible to find a place to relax in comfort. In the squares, there is a bit of a carnival atmosphere. As in many public areas throughout the world, street performers try to bewitch the crowd with their acts, whether they be magic or mime.

Near the National Garden lies the Panathenaic Stadium, the stadium at which the Olympic Games were renewed in 1896. The Greeks were dismayed to lose the 1996 Olympic Games—the hundredth anniversary in modern times—to the American city of Atlanta, Georgia, feeling, of course, that such a momentous centenary should be celebrated in its original home.

Syntagma Square is flanked by many luxury hotels, including the stately Hotel Grande Bretagne. The hotel was originally built in 1842 as a guest house for palace visitors. It became a public hotel in 1874. For shoppers, the stores off Syntagma Square are a bounteous trove. Shoes of all kinds can be found within a few blocks of the square, as well as jewellry modelled on Cycladic designs, the boutiques of famous designers, and specialty shops.

Near Syntagma Square is one of the oldest parts of town, known as the Plaka. In

*The National Museum of Athens contains many examples
of Greek art and antiquities from throughout its history.
Here are seen two bas-relief from its collections.*

Evzones standing guard in front of the Tomb of the Unknown Soldier is one of the most remarkable sights in Athens. The colourfully garbed soldiers salute each other on the hour, but otherwise make no motion; nor do they acknowledge the tourists and rascals who try to distract them.

The Royal Palace, on the border of Syntagma Square, was the former home of kings. The last king, Constantine, fled during the military junta of 1967; the palace now houses the Greek Parliament.

the Plaka one finds a timelessness which is also contemporary. Many of the buildings date from the nineteenth century, yet are filled with modern shops, bustling tavernas, *mezedopolia* (restaurants that serve appetisers), and roof gardens. The walls of the buildings are brightly painted with murals that describe what's supposed to be going on inside.

The stores of the Plaka are filled with everything from traditional wares, walls of what appear to be identical leather sandals and purses, to designer clothing and folk art, and souvenir shops devoted to those ubiquitous photographic models, 'the cats of Greece'.

Within the Plaka's precincts it is also possible to see some older buildings—churches dating back to the Byzantine era, and one remarkable architectural feature remaining from first-century BC Athens: the Tower of the Winds.

The Plaka is a welter of humanity, with wall-to-wall tourists, merchants, and taverna barkers who implore the crowds to come see Greek dancing. Cats, whose tourist appeal cannot be denied, are underfoot, graciously accepting proffered food and disdainfully cadging it when none is offered. Even the local cinema appears timeless, housed in its nineteenth-century building of yellowed stone. At night, the vivacity of the ebullient Greek spirit is everywhere in evidence, with crowded restaurants and discotheques spilling their music and laughter into the streets.

Although many are of two minds regarding the national cuisine, there's no denying the delectability of the vividly coloured vegetables. Clams and oysters, often on display on ice-packed tables outside the restaurants, are sometimes so fresh they squirt passersby with sea water.

The Theatre of Dionysus, which dates from the Classical period, is also near the Plaka. There the plays of the great tragedians of ancient Greece—Aeschylus, Sophocles, and Euripides—as well as the comedies of Aristophanes—were first heard and judged by the Athenian populace.

Items found in various archaeological digs include coins. This silver tetrhorachin from the fifth century BC is of Athenian mintage; it may have been found in the ancient Athenian Agora, where excavations have been ongoing since the 1930s.

The Monastiraki Quarter is, like the Plaka, one of the most picturesque areas of Athens. Originally the old Turkish quarter, Monastiraki has a famous flea market which is an absolute must-see for visitors.

The Plaka, a neighbourhood of nineteenth-century buildings, is one of the most lively areas in Athens, filled with tavernas, cafes, shops, nightclubs and—on any given night—enormous crowds.

Classical Athens gave a lasting legacy to the dramatic arts. Tragedy and comedy, as they developed in Athens, added voices and characters to the traditional chorus, and thus was born the modern play.

Ancient Greek tragedies—less so comedy—are so accessible and appealing to modern audiences that they are still performed today. In ancient times, the plays were presented at the Dionysian festival, with awards going to the best playwright. The three tragedians whose works endure in complete form today are Sophocles, Aeschylus, and Euripides. The importance of these three is stressed in a comedy play, *The Frogs*, written by Aristophanes, the only comedian whose work has come down to us. These were masterful artists, recognised as such in their own time. At one point Sophocles, who was accused of senility by his sons, was acquitted by a jury when he submitted his work-in-progress, *Oedipus at Colonus*, as evidence. Euripides's fame reached as far as Macedonia—then considered 'barbaric'—and he was invited to the court of Archelaos. It could be that enthusiasm for all things Greek ran in the blood of the Macedonians, since Philip of Macedon engaged Aristotle to tutor his son, Alexander, who was perhaps the greatest Hellenophile of all.

Folk and arts festivals have long been appreciated in Athens, with thousands in attendance. Such performances are held during the summer at the Odeum Herodes Atticus, a second-century BC theatre.

If, while strolling about the city, you notice lapses in the continuity of Athenian architecture, it is because Athens suffered a decline for several centuries, from the Byzantine Empire through the Ottoman rule. Only in modern history did Athens revive as the capital of Greek spirit. Thus, the majority of houses date from the nineteenth century onward, with a few appearances of antique and Byzantine jewels.

One such antique manifestation is the Athenian Agora, where ancient stones of Athens bear mute testimony

Athens has a thoroughly modern mass-transit system, as evidenced by this photograph. Subways carry passengers throughout the city, even as far as Athens' port, Piraeus.

Piraeus is the port of Athens. In Classical times, a wall was built to shield traffic to and from the city from attack. Now Piraeus is connected to Athens by mass transit and roadways; it is still the busiest port in Greece, with ships and ferries leading to the islands and other ports of call.

to the past. In 1967, one was found which was simply inscribed, 'I am the boundary of the Agora'. It was the second boundary marker to have been discovered in sixty years of excavating the site.

The Agora was the heart of Classical Athens. It was where the populace of Athens met to ostracise the powerful—a potsherd with Pericles' name on it tells that story. It was there also that Socrates held his seat in the Assembly, taught philosophy on the steps of the Stoa of Zeus, and was arrested at the Royal Stoa. The foundations of these structures, along with the sites where the Assembly met—including a humble cobbler's shop—have been unearthed and are now open to public view.

Strange as it may seem, the Agora was lost to time for fourteen centuries, and only rediscovered in the 1930s. Even now, excavations can still yield revelations. The famous Painted Stoa, presumed lost forever, was uncovered in the Agora as late as 1981.

Slightly elevated at the edge of the Agora is the Hephaistion, a Doric temple dedicated to the god Hephaistos. It has survived the ruins of time extremely well, and looks almost modern beside the excavated rubble.

It's easy to see why the Athenians are so proud of their city: it is eternal, and to walk its timeless streets is to be, like the city itself, renewed.

Athens is a convenient base for day trips, which might include the ancient site of the Mysteries at Eleusis or newer mysteries at the Monastery of Dafni. Also close by is the port of Piraeus. In its harbour are boats ready and willing to take visitors to any point in the Greek islands; at the Cape of Sounion, east of Athens on the tip of the Attic peninsula, is a beautiful Classical temple dedicated to Poseidon, erected by the people of ancient Athens. Looking down from the temple into the vivid blue waters, it is almost possible to imagine Pericles' proud fleet once more sailing by.

The Temple of Poseidon, like many ancient ruins (including the Acropolis), has been emblazoned by the graffiti of travellers wishing to commemorate their visit. Here is the inscription of none other than the poet Lord Byron, who succumbed to death in Greece during its war of independence.

After Athena, the sea god Poseidon was the most important deity to the Classical Athenians, whose sea power extended their empire and made them the masters of the Mediterranean until the Peloponnesian Wars (431-404 BC).

Churches and temples are often built on the site of other buildings. The Temple of Poseidon is no exception, having been built upon previous, Archaic temples dedicated to both Poseidon and Athena.

*Piraeus, long known as the port of Athens, is now a bustling town on its
own, whose draw to tourists includes its ferries and its seafood restaurants.
The low, terraced buildings pictured here have a view of the port.*

*The Temple of Poseidon
at Cape Sounion was built in
the fifth century BC. Like the
Parthenon, it was part of
Pericles's building scheme.*

The Peloponnesos

*T*he Peloponnesos perhaps contains the most complete historical account of the Greek nation. Traces of settlements dating back as far as Neolithic times can be found and ancient civilisations have surfaced with regularity. Legendary enemies have risen and fallen and the glories of empires have come and gone into dust upon its fertile plains. But what seems most significant when one considers the Peloponnesos is that it is the land of Homer's Achaeans and of the Classical Spartans. Unlike Attica however, the history of the Peloponnesos is almost completely documented; it was never lost to time.

The Peloponnesian peninsula was settled by an ancient culture called Mycenae, whose merchants traded all over the ancient world. This culture inexplicably collapsed. Then, about 1000 BC, invaders from the north known as Dorians arrived, conquering the peninsula and creating the cultures that evolved into the Classical period.

In more recent times, the Romans vanquished the Peloponnesos and made it an outpost of the empire. It was then conquered in the thirteenth century by the Venetians, who held it against the Turks until the seventeenth century.

The historic name of this peninsula originates in the depths of time with Pelops, who originally claimed it as 'the island of Pelops'. From the work of the great tragedian Aeschylus, many are familiar with the 'curse of the House of Atreus'. According to legend, Pelops was the ill-fated son of the notorious King Tantalus, who killed and dismembered him and then served him to the gods to see if they were all-knowing. Although the gods brought Pelops back to life and punished his father, bad blood seemed to run in the family (Pelops himself was

cursed by a man he betrayed), and misfortune followed them all the way down to Orestes who, pursued by the Furies for murdering his father, Agamemnon, was finally expiated in Athens, thus bringing the family's tragic cycle to an end.

Although the whole of the Peloponnesos is well worth seeing, the following are a few of its most remarkable, not-to-be-missed sites.

Corinth and its Canal

In the time of Pelops, indeed, almost until the present day, the Peloponnesos was not an island at all but a broad peninsula attached to the mainland by a narrow isthmus, where the city of Corinth stands. Ships wishing to pass from the Ionian to the Aegean were carried by labourers along a path that ran across the neck of the peninsula, and were charged exorbitantly for the privilege by the Corinthians.

Corinth was destroyed numerous times by the ravages of war and earthquake; since 1896, excavations on the site of the ancient city have been conducted to discover more about the Corinthians when they were at their height.

The Argolid town of Nauplion is now a bustling tourist center, thanks to its spectacular setting on the Gulf of Argolis. In the past, the gulf attracted such imperial-minded conquerors as the Venetians, who held it from the late 14th century until the Turkish conquest in 1540.

Ancient Corinth was a wealthy place because of trading and tolls; it was also exceptional for its temple dedicated to Aphrodite-Astarte, where a thousand priestesses welcomed worshippers in a manner befitting the Goddesses of Love. It is impossible to say exactly what the city was like in its heyday, although there have been ongoing excavations since 1896. The ancient city was destroyed by earthquakes and sacked by the Romans. Even into this century, earthquakes have plagued the site. What can be seen is the Acrocorinth built by the Romans, looming above the modern city below. All that remains of the Greek habitation is part of the old marketplace, a temple dedicated to Apollo, and a fountain which was preserved by the Romans.

Probably the idea for a canal at the Corinthian isthmus came from the first man who either hauled his ship overland or sailed past the dangerous capes of Taenarus and Malaea far to the south, but it is attributed to the Corinthian tyrant, Periander, in 600 BC. Implementation of a plan, however, waited for the infamous Roman Emperor Nero, who is said to have dug the first spadeful of the canal himself in AD 97 and carried it back to Rome with him. However, with the fall of Nero, the half-finished canal languished for centuries until it was completed by the French in 1893, who consulted, among other things, the original Roman plan.

Today one might pass through the canal, which is extremely narrow, with sheer walls carved out of hard rock, climbing a good distance, and come to such places as the legendary Mycenae.

Mycenae

Visitors to the Peloponnesos are almost invariably directed to the excavations at Mycenae, the site housing the remains of one of the oldest civilisations in the world, and certainly one of those most inspiring to the Western world. Mycenae was the ancient kingdom of the Achaeans, considered by

historians to be the people who warred against the city of Troy in Homer's epic poem, the *Iliad*.

Mycenae was first excavated by the redoubtable amateur archaeologist Heinrich Schliemann. As a child, Schliemann was inspired by Homer's epics. Later, he became obsessed with proving their veracity by discovering the site of Troy. Using his own money, and having acquired a Greek wife to teach him the modern language, he began to prospect for Troy at the age of forty-one and, amazingly, discovered the actual site in 1870.

Having achieved extraordinary success with Troy, Schliemann then came to the Peloponnesos to find Mycenae itself, the kingdom of Agamemnon. In 1876, he found ruins dating back to 1250 BC and before. Schliemann excavated the beehive-shaped structure called the Treasury Building (also called the Treasury of Atreus and Tomb of Agamemnon), exposed the now-famous Lion's Gate, and exhumed the grave circle, which is said to have been of the Mycenaean kings and the stones surrounding their tombstones. Mycenaean royalty were buried in a standing position, their faces covered with golden masks. Subsequent digs have uncovered an oil merchant's shop and other finds.

Another discovery made at Mycenae was that of the Phaistos disk. While less impressive than other treasures, the Phaistos disk provided the key that unlocked the identity of the ancient Mycenaeans. It was inscribed with a written language, known as 'Linear B', which was also found on many tablets at the Minoan sites on Crete. At the time, it was hypothesised that these two cultures were of Phoenician origin. When deciphered by the team of Ventris and Chadwick in the middle of this century, the disk proved beyond a doubt that the ancient Achaeans were the forerunners of the Hellenes.

The site of the Sea Kings' kingdom now stands empty and overgrown, yawning with its treasures long

Sparse but elegant ruins give the visitor an idea of the beauty of ancient Corinth. Pictured are first-century ruins: at the edge of the old market-place is the entrance to a shop; in the background stands a temple dedicated to Apollo.

removed. Still, visitors may pass through the Lion's Gate, which is built of colossal blocks of stone, look out onto the sea or to the fertile plain, and imagine the glory of Mycenae when Agamemnon and his Achaeans sailed out to the coast of Asia Minor in defence of his brother's honour.

Pilos

Other ruins dating back to Mycenaean times can be found at Pilos in the southern Peloponnesos—the 'sandy Pilos' of Homeric legend. There stands a palace which some have attributed to Nestor, the eldest king of the Achaeans and Agamemnon's counsellor.

Other buildings at Pylos, such as the old Venetian fortress (called Paleokastro, or 'old fortress') and a fifteenth-century Turkish one (the Neokastro), mark notches in the history of Greece's occupation. Pilos is also famous for two critical military engagements: the first took place in the fourth century BC, when four hundred Spartans defied the Athenians during the Peloponnesian War; second was the naval defeat of Ibrahim Pasha in 1827, which decided the outcome of the Greeks' War of Independence.

Sparta

Today, the placid Arcadian plain upon which the sleepy town of Sparta reaps its crops belies the tremendous militaristic civilisation that was once the terror of Athens. The Classical Spartans believed themselves descended from northern tribes called Dorians, who overran the Peloponnesos around 1000 BC in what archaeologists term the 'Dorian invasion'. The evidence that this invasion actually occurred is found in a number of pots, called 'Barbarian ware', which have been discovered near Sparta and other parts of the Peloponnesos, as well as in northwest Greece.

Throughout the fifth and fourth centuries BC, Sparta was the enemy of Athens. The two city-states clashed in battle time and again, the most memorable being the Peloponnesian Wars (431-404 BC) and the Corinthian War (395-386 BC). While the imperialistic ambitions demonstrated by both Athens and Sparta were not unalike, there could not be a greater spiritual contrast. Unlike Athens, which had evolved its democratic form of government in the early fifth century BC, Sparta's government was rooted in Mycenaean and Doric traditions, a hereditary dual kingship, and a constitution devised by

The ruins of this spring and bath date back only as far as the Roman occupation of Corinth. Little is seen of the city in its ancient heyday.

Heinrich Schliemann, amateur archaeologist extraordinaire, excavated the beehive-shaped Treasury Building of Mycenae in 1876. The building's other names—the Treasury of Atreus and Tomb of Agamemnon—bespeak those figures of Homeric legend which led him to search and find his childhood dreams.

the legendary lawgiver Lycourgos. It had not changed for centuries. The Spartans' rigidity, coupled with their superior military prowess, ultimately defeated the Athenians. Under Spartan domination, the light of Athens dimmed, never to return to its former glory.

The end of Spartan rule arrived with the kingship of Agesilaos, which lasted from 400 to 360 BC. Agesilaos' reign was plagued by unrest from the Helots (an indigenous people who were treated like serfs) within and the rest of the Hellenes and the Persians without. As years of fighting had emptied Sparta of the able-bodied men needed to defend its empire, the Corinthian War tolled its death-knell.

Curiously, there is little to show of these remarkable people, for the sparse ruins of Sparta do not tell the story of its great rise and fall. Looking out upon the present agricultural nature of the site, one might be tempted to say that swords were beaten into ploughshares.

Mistra

Mistra was once a capital city of the Byzantine Empire, but like Sparta, its glory has come and gone, and only a few churches remain amid the seasonal riot of flowers.

The Crusader Guillaume de Villehardouin originally built a French fortress here in the mid-thirteenth century, but he was forced to relinquish Mistra to the Greeks as a ransom. It became a Byzantine fortress town, and continued to flourish up until the seventeenth century under different conquerors, the last being the Turks.

The city, during its brief respite of Byzantine rule in the fourteenth century, saw a renaissance of Byzantine culture. Its glory included the habitation of the Christian philosopher Theophilus, and culminated with the crowning of Constantine Palaeologus there in 1449—the last Byzantine Emperor.

Among the remaining buildings from that time is the famous Monastery of Pantanassa. The monastery can be easily seen against the steep mountainside, overshadowed by a Frankish fort. Visitors may gasp at the beauty of the light admitted through its many-windowed dome, and enjoy its vaults, which have beautiful frescoes dating from the fourteenth and fifteenth centuries. Efforts were undertaken to renovate the monastery in the nineteenth century, but time again has caught up with the structure.

Other treasures of Mistra include the churches of Saint Demetrios Peribleptos, as well as Saint George's Church, the site of the last Byzantine coronation.

Nauplion

Nauplion is one of those picture-perfect Greek towns. Situated upon a rocky finger thrusting itself into the Gulf of Argolis, it provides a unique and beautiful view of both blue water and the adjoining Peloponnesian coast.

With its natural harbour, and convenient location on the Greek mainland, Nauplion has long been a stronghold for naval imperialists. In the third century BC, the town was protected by a number of forts, which can still be found guarding the city below after all these centuries. The city also boasts several Venetian fortresses, attesting to the

Contemporary tourists entering and departing through the Lion's Gate of the ancient city of Mycenae (1250 BC) indicate the grand scale on which the Sea Kings' empire was built.

centuries-long sovereignty of the Peloponnesos.

Today, Nauplion remains a bustling port, although a great deal of its trade is in tourism. Although the city presents a predominantly modern face, part of its past can be glimpsed in its cemetery, where ancient cedars stand as watchful sentinels.

Epidaurus

Every year, Greek nationals and tourists alike visit the ancient pine groves of Epidaurus to take part in a centuries-old ritual. There, they seat themselves in the amphitheatre of Epidaurus, where under the stars and with perfect acoustics, they enjoy Classical plays that are now performed in modern Greek.

Built in the fourth century BC, the amphitheatre has been restored and is presently the site of a seasonal festival. There, the massive whiteness and perfect circularity of its stage awe visitors, who have commented on the feeling of historical authenticity inspired by the experience of attending the festival.

Perhaps their inspiration has to do with the site itself. Epidaurus was home to Asclepias the healer. Like Heracles, Asclepias had demi-god status; his famous sanctuary, the Asclepion, was visited by all who sought answers to their health problems. Within the Asclepion was the Abaton, where invalids awaited answers in their dreams, and a 160-bed Katagogion, where they often remained to recuperate from their ill health.

Like many holy places, the Asclepion was built upon a site long considered to be holy ground. The sanctuary itself was erected over the site of a shrine to Apollo Mateas, dating back to the seventh century BC.

The Palamedes fortress, which still looms above Nauplion from the height of the coastal cliffs, was named for a hero in the Trojan War.

Argos

Located just north of Nauplion, Argos is one of the oldest habitations in the Peloponnesos, dating back to perhaps the Neolithic age. The fertile Argive plain has certainly seen human habitation since the earliest times. However, except for the Mycenean ruins at Tiryns to the east, Argos is very much a small but bustling trading city. Some evidence remains of Argos' occupation by the Romans, as witnessed by the well-preserved, nearly complete Roman baths and aqueduct. Also remaining are the Greek fourth-century amphitheatre that can seat twenty thousand, and the Venetian fortress, which was in such good condition that it served the Greeks as a defence against the Turks during the nineteenth-century War of Independence.

Olympia

After Athens, Olympia, located on the northwest part of the Peloponnesian peninsula, is probably the most famous name of antiquity. There are indications that it was of great sanctity as early as 1600 BC, and certainly considered hallowed by the eighth century BC. The site is still marvelous, along the valley of the Alpheus, and the quiet hills seem timeless. Still, they must have roared with the cheers of the crowds in ancient times. Every four years at Olympia, beginning in 776 BC, the Greek city-states would set aside their differences and participate in the Olympic Games, which were famous throughout the country and widely attended.

Hydra's tiny port is very picturesque, with whitewashed buildings covered by shallow, squarish roofs. They must already start to climb the steep mountainside, even though they are at water's edge.

Like all games and festivals of the ancient world, the Olympic Games had religious significance, but also came to signify the Greek philosophy that the most admirable individual was the one who excelled both physically and mentally. Winners of the games gained extraordinary renown and were praised by poet and patron alike.

Since each city-state naturally hoped that their athletes would win, each poured its wealth into the environs of Olympia in the hopes of propitiating the gods to use their influence to determine the outcome of an event. The major deity of the site was Zeus, but many others were also considered to be present and have influence. Thus, Olympia became a site of vast wealth, and even now, after the plundering of centuries, excavation may still yield up new treasures.

Among the structures which can be found at Olympia are the ruins of the Temple of Zeus, built in the fifth century BC and one of the largest temples in Greece. The depiction of the Seer on its eastern pediment was

This photograph shows the narrowness of the canal of Corinth, as well as the height of the rock which was sheared to create it. The canal was originally begun by the Emperor Nero in AD 97, but was completed by the French in 1893.

Like Athens, Olympia was one of the most important centres in the Classical world. It was here that the city-nations and leagues which made up the Hellenes would set aside their differences to participate in the Olympic Games.

The fortress of Palamedes, which stands high above the town of Nauplion, was built in the third century BC. Nauplion was a strategic naval point along the Argolid coast.

considered unusual because of its physical imperfections of sagging belly and deeply furrowed brow, a seemingly strange choice to adorn a site which praised physical perfection. Others include a pair of seventh-century BC Doric temples dedicated to the Mother of the Gods and Hera, as well as a number of treasuries and athletic buildings. The fourth-century BC stadium could accommodate forty thousand spectators, which gives some idea of the popularity of the Games.

Among the well-known statuary found at Olympia were Praxiteles's Hermes and Dionysus, the Nike of Paeonius, and Apollo judging the Battle of the Centaurs and Lapiths. Lost has been Phidias's statue of Zeus, inlaid with gold and ivory, said to be one of the Seven Wonders of the World.

The Olympic Games were suspended in the fourth century AD, then time and earthquakes took charge of the site until its rediscovery in the eighteenth century. In the nineteenth century, the Olympic Games were reinstated, but were moved to Athens.

Bassae

The Temple of Bassae, which was Doric in design, was dedicated to Apollo Epicourios—'Apollo of Timely Aid'. It was reputedly designed by Ictinus in the fifth century BC, and was in almost perfect condition when it was discovered by the French architect Joachim Baucher in 1765, who was touring the countryside south of Olympia. As ancient as it was, the temple still possessed its remarkable frieze depicting the battle of the Centaurs and Lapiths.

The temple belies its name, since Baucher, its rescuer, was murdered in a subsequent trip to preserve it. The temple was eventually excavated in 1812, with the architect Haller van Hallstein sketching every block. This was fortunate, since the temple was then dismantled and claimed by the museums of just about every country in Europe.

Although its friezes and metopes—vividly realised—finally ended up in the British Museum, the temple itself remains remarkably intact, despite its brushes with the hand of man and nature. It is an eye-catching sight, set as it is in the midst of gently rolling hills.

The amphitheatre of Epidaurus, with its breathtaking location and perfect acoustics, is having a renaissance. Built in the fourth century BC, the amphitheatre has been restored and is the site of a seasonal festival, where Classical plays are performed in modern Greek.

Northern and Central Greece

*T*he mainland of Greece is composed of the northern regions of Thrace, Macedonia, and Thessaly, which includes several famous monasteries as well as the sacred Mount Olympos (the legendary home of the gods); the northwestern region known as Epirus; and the central region—the peninsula which ends in the region of Attica—where can be found, among other destinations, the ancient site of Delphi. The northern and western regions of Greece border several Slavic states as well as Turkey, and are host to a variety of cultural influences. Despite this, it was the northern reaches of Macedonia to which produced the most determined proponent of Greekness: Alexander the Great.

Macedonia

Greek Macedonia, the region of Greece bordered by Albania, Bulgaria, and the former Yugoslavia, has an illustrious history. Famous as the birthplace of Alexander the Great, it was this ancient city-state, while considered 'unsophisticated' by Classical Athenian standards, that was the driving force behind bringing Hellenic culture to the world.

Although it was the conquests of Alexander, lasting from 336 until his death in 323 BC, that universally promulgated Hellenism, it was Archilaos (d. 399 BC) who first sought to enlighten his own people, by inviting the great names of Athens, Euripides among them, to visit the region. After Archilaos, it was Alexander's father, Philip II (359-336 BC), who succeeded in unifying the Greeks—although only by conquering them first. Alexander followed his example, extending his empire as far east as India.

The tiny settlements of the Thessalian plain seem to cower in the shadow of the Meteora, the unreal hills which jut out of the northern landscape.

But Alexander's wasn't the only Macedonian empire known to history—only the first. In the eleventh century, a Macedonian named Basil II (called the 'Bulgar-Slayer') took the throne of the Byzantine Empire; and defeated the Bulgarians who (along with several other northern tribes) had at that time settled the better part of Greece. Although his dynasty lasted barely two hundred years, it held the borders of empire for a time, and fostered a renaissance of Byzantine art and architecture.

Macedonia is in many respects unlike the rest of Greece. It is considerably colder, near freezing in the winter months and rainy in the summer. Yet, like the rest of Greece, it is rich in archaeological finds, not the least of which was the 1977 discovery at Vergina of the cremated remains of the great Philip II. As the excavations show, Philip apparently was buried in a state befitting a conqueror: in an elaborate tomb, adorned with painted frescoes and quantities of gold.

The Sanctuary of Athena Pronaea stands in lonely splendour nearby Delphi. Built in the fourth century BC, the temple's tholos was composed of twenty outer columns and ten inner ones, forming an arcade.

Pella, near where the modern city of Edessa now stands, is the legendary birthplace of Alexander. The city itself dates back to the fourth century BC, and was once the capital of Classical Macedonia. On display in the city museum are a number of treasures, including seven mosaic floors dating from around 300 BC, depicting mythical hunting and battle scenes.

Macedonia is crisscrossed with mountain ranges, such as the dark-firred Pindus mountains and the Rhodope range. It is considerably greener than southern Greece, and has many breathtakingly beautiful areas, such as the placid Lake Orestias in the northwest, near the city of Castoria.

The economy of Macedonia is overwhelmingly agricultural, with the principal export being tobacco. The majority of tobacco is shipped from the port of Kavalla in the northeast. Other staples are various grains—rye, barley, wheat, and corn—and, of course, vineyards that produce Macedonian wine.

Macedonia is more culturally diverse than southern Greece, bordering as it does four Balkan countries—indeed, having been part of these countries at different times. One ethnic group, the Sarakatsani, has interesting traditional costumes made of wool woven into intricate patterns of bright colours. The women sometimes wear elaborate headdresses.

The ancient theatre at Delphi is small but acoustically perfect. The Classical plays are now enacted in a seasonal festival, bringing the past to life for visitors.

At Delphi, the Treasury of the Athenians has been partially restored. It had been found in pieces on the ground. Its columns were knocked over by earthquakes and shorn of their marble by thieves long ago.

*Previous page:
The treasure house
of the Athenians
at Delphi is an
example of how
the ancient Greeks
built storehouses
on sacred sites
for reasons of reli-
gion and status.*

*The Meteora monastic complex is a
virtual treasury of early Christian art;
here, a fresco from the fourteenth-century
Macedonian school graces the wall,
showing Christ in the centre, flanked
by His mother, Mary, and St John.*

*Near Delphi, Arahova is a pic-
turesque town in the Parnassus
region of Greece, with its whitewashed, red-roofed houses perched
along the mountain's craggy sides.
Arahova's vineyards are famous for
the sweet, resinous wine, kokinelli.*

Thrace

Thrace, the northernmost part of Greece, is bounded by Turkey and Bulgaria. The area is still largely rural, little developed, and home to many nomadic peoples of diverse ethnic backgrounds. In the towns of Xante and Komotini, it is possible to observe residents attired in their traditional costume, which is of Turkish origin.

In this hilly, mountainous region, goat and sheep herding are chief among livelihoods, and goat meat, milk, and cheese are stored up against the coming of winter and hard times.

Along the Thracian coast lies the port town of Kavala. The Byzantine fortress which overlooks Kavala bears witness to the enormous influence the Byzantine Empire once wielded here, before it was overtaken by a series of European invaders and, finally, the Turks.

Along the Thracian coast lies Kavala, a beautiful small town. The Venetian fortress which overlooks Kavala bears witness to the enormous influence the Venetians wielded from the end of the Byzantine era onward.

This Greek shepherd is relaxing before it's time to milk the goats. The Greek countryside is dependent upon the goat for meat and milk, and cheese-making is a household chore.

In the north, nomadic peoples such as the Sarakatsani have lived for centuries by having as many goats as will prosper upon the land.

The northern reaches of Greece are still home to many nomadic peoples of diverse ethnic backgrounds. In Thrace, this shepherd's hut made of reeds, in the traditional Sarakatsani style, bears witness to the persistence of ancestral ways.

These fourth-century Roman walls, which once enclosed the city of Thessaloniki (then Salonika), bespeak of its time as a far-flung outpost of the Roman Empire.

Thessaloniki

Like Athens, Thessaloniki is a contemporary metropolis with memories of earlier times. But unlike Athens, whose founding is so ancient as to be a matter of legend, Thessaloniki was founded in 315 BC by the Macedonian king Cassander, who named it after his wife, Salonika, the sister of Alexander the Great.

As with most of the ancient world, Salonika endured Roman occupation. Great stone walls, built in the fourth century, which once enclosed the city and the Arch of Galerius, built in 303, bear testimony to the presence of the Romans.

For the most part, however, Thessaloniki plainly displays its Byzantine heritage. Having prospered as a port and as a centre of culture during the Byzantine Empire, particularly during the tenth and eleventh centuries, Thessaloniki in that time surpassed Athens as Greece's most influential city, and was second to Constantinople in significance.

In Christian history, Thessaloniki is notable for Saint Paul's visit in AD 46, an event which inspired him to write his *Letter to the Thessalonicians*, which is included in the New Testament. This is not to say that the Thessalonicians were easily won; Roman emperor Galerius severely persecuted the Christian population, putting to death a certain Demetrios, who subsequently became the city's patron saint and a worker of many miracles.

In spite of its importance to Christianity, Thessaloniki is also a city of religious tolerance. When Ferdinand and Isabella expelled the Jews from Spain during the fifteenth century, many of them came to Thessaloniki, where there already was a large Jewish population. This segment of Thessaloniki continues to thrive as a necessary part of that city's tradition.

Today, Thessaloniki is a populous city stretching along the coast of the Aegean. It is the second-busiest port of Greece (after Piraeus) and it is beginning to enjoy a larger percentage of tourism.

Reasons for visiting Thessaloniki are numerous. The Quay of Vasileos Constantinou juts out into a beautiful harbour. Relatively tall buildings (for Greece) with colourful awnings line the busy street that runs along its seawall, framing a quaint view. Restaurants offer delicious seafood fresh from the Aegean, and architectural gems from the Byzantine era abound. For example, one might visit the church of Aghia Sophia, built during the short-lived eleventh-century renaissance; the Church of the Holy Apostles, with its mosaic of Christ Pantocrator; and the fifth-century Panaghia Ahiropiitos, where a miraculous icon of the Virgin—not painted by human hands—once reportedly appeared.

In Thessaloniki, the famous Arch built by Emperor Galerius in AD 297 stands amid contemporary buildings. Much more remains of Thessaloniki's Byzantine legacy, when it surpassed Athens to become the capital of Greece.

The best Greek fare is noted for its freshness. Here, a plate of shrimp, caught in the Aegean near Thessaloniki, makes the mouth water.

Although the people of Greece are predominantly Greek Orthodox, there is some religious diversity, mostly in cities and in the north. In Thessaloniki in particular there is a large Jewish population. Here, a bar mitzvah celebration is taking place.

Travellers often visit Greece in the summertime—when the land is baked by the relentless sun—and then go only to Athens and the islands. Doing so, they miss the spectacular spring, when fields—such as these in Thessaloniki—burst into riotous colour.

Delphi

Delphi is one of the most sacred places in Greece. Thought by the Greeks to be the centre of the world, a giant, carved boulder was placed there to signify the *omphalos*—'navel' in Greek—of Delphi. The site and its oracle had certainly had religious significance for centuries before Apollo assumed guardianship, and games and festivals (called the Pythian games, after the female mouthpiece of the oracle) were held to commemorate its sacred importance.

Kings and commoners both came to consult the oracle, and each propitiated Apollo in some way. Individual votive offerings have been excavated, but treasure-houses built by city-states are the most obvious structures of propitiation. Of these, the treasure-house of the Siphnians is one of the best preserved; it still possesses its original friezes upon which scenes from Greek mythology are discernible. Unfortunately, the Sanctuary of Apollo has not endured well. Its few remaining columns—those that have not been destroyed by earthquake or plundering—have been resurrected, and stand near the bottom of the ancient theatre.

Within the sanctuary is the spring of Kastalia. An abundant and sacred water, it feeds the sanctuary's pools, and plunges out of the rock in a natural fountain.

Near Delphi is the town of Arahova, where it is possible to linger and enjoy *kokinelli*, the sweet, resinous wine grown in its vineyards.

The spring of Kastalia was also sacred in Delphi. Once the source of the sacred pools of Delphi, it still bubbles timelessly out of the ground.

Christians once tried to claim the sacred spring of Kastalia by building their own shrine nearby; however, the site was destined to be forever pagan.

In Greece, where the olive has long been sacred, nowhere could be a better explanation for its reverence than this grove of four-hundred-year-old olive trees nears Delphi.

Pictured here is the sculptured navel stone (omphalos in Greek) of Delphi. It symbolises the ancient Greeks' belief that Delphi was the centre of the world. The site was certainly important, for it was here that king and commoner alike sought answers from the Pythia—the woman through whom the gods spoke.

Many beautiful mosaics were pried up and taken to grace the floors of Greece's many conquerors; however, this particular one has remained among the Delphic ruins for centuries.

As ancient as the Sanctuary of Athena Pronaea is, it sits upon the foundations of an even older temple, built in the sixth century BC.

The Monasteries Of Mount Athos And Meteora

During the turbulent times of early Christianity and the Byzantine era, monasteries were the calm in the eye of the storm. And as seclusion and monasticism were tenets of the early Christian Church (as was their opposite, evangelicalism), it was only natural that some priests would seek seclusion within a monastic system.

The first Greek Orthodox monastery was built at Mount Athos, on the isolated Chalkidiki peninsula in northern Greece, by Saint Ossios Athanassios in the tenth century. The original monastery of Megisti Lavra, on the peninsula's tip, soon became part of a complex of monasteries which, at its height during the Byzantine era, contained forty separate monasteries and forty thousand monks. Today, the number of monasteries is down to twenty, and only ten men from the outside—whose credentials are scrupulously checked—are allowed to visit at any given time. These structures, in place since the eleventh century, were laid down by the Emperor Constantine Monomachos; they also stipulate that women are not allowed to visit Mount Athos—ever. In fact, ships with women passengers must come no closer to the coast than 500 feet (152 metres).

The Mount Athos monastic complex is self-governing; like the Vatican, it is a law unto itself. It protects and preserves a vast collection of Byzantine art, including murals dating from the fourteenth century, frescoes by Byzantine masters, rich icons, and many priceless books. The Cloister of

The Meteora shelters a complex of monasteries, the oldest of which—the Grand Meteoron— was built in the early fourteenth century. These monasteries remain a bastion of Greek Orthodox belief to this day, as well as a treasury of religious art and a magnet for tourists.

Monasteries are typically built into almost inaccessible reaches, and therefore touring them requires stamina. Here, visitors ascend to the fourteenth-century Monastery of Ossios Varlaam.

Previous page:
The Monastery
of Ossios Varlaam,
a fourteenth-
century monastery
that is part of
the Meteora
monastic complex,
is built high the
mountains, and
overlooks the
Thessalian plain.

Dionysus, a wooden structure that juts out from the side of the mountain like an eagle's aerie.

Another well-known Greek Orthodox monastery is the Meteora, situated upon the strangely shaped mountains which jut from the Thessalian plain, near the town of Kalambaka. The Meteora also shelters a complex of monasteries, the oldest of which—Grand Meteoron—was built in the late fourteenth century and swiftly followed by five others. As with Mount Athos, the Meteora remains a bastion of Greek Orthodox belief, as well as a treasury of religious art. The Meteora monastic complex will admit any visitors, including women, who are conservatively dressed—this includes a head covering as well as long sleeves and a long skirt—and have the stamina to climb up to its almost inaccessible reaches.

The Meteora monastic complex contains six monasteries: the Monastery of Saint Nicholas Anapafasas, Ossios Varlaam, the Grand Meteoron, Roussanou and Holy Trinity (which are convents), and Saint Stephanos. The complex is a virtual hoard of early Christian art, containing frescoes, icons, rare books, and some unusual items of holy life, such as a necropolis made up of the skulls of former monks.

The monks and nuns, though used to visitors, maintain the discipline which has called them to this unusual life and made it possible for them to endure isolation.

A monk ringing
bells in the
Monastery of
Ossios Varlaam.
In these monaster-
ies, most of which
date from the thir-
teenth and four-
teenth centuries,
daily rituals have
barely changed.

Icons represent some of the most stunning expressions of religious feeling, as one can see in this icon of St Andreas (ca. 1665-1675), which is showered with gold and artistic detail. Nonetheless, icons prompted turbulent accusations of idolatry; it is a controversy far from over.

Here, a monk of the Monastery of Ossios Varlaam operates a windlass. The Greek Orthodox religion has its roots in the earliest Christian beliefs; part of the New Testament—that of St John—was written in koine, a common Greek dialect used throughout the Roman Empire.

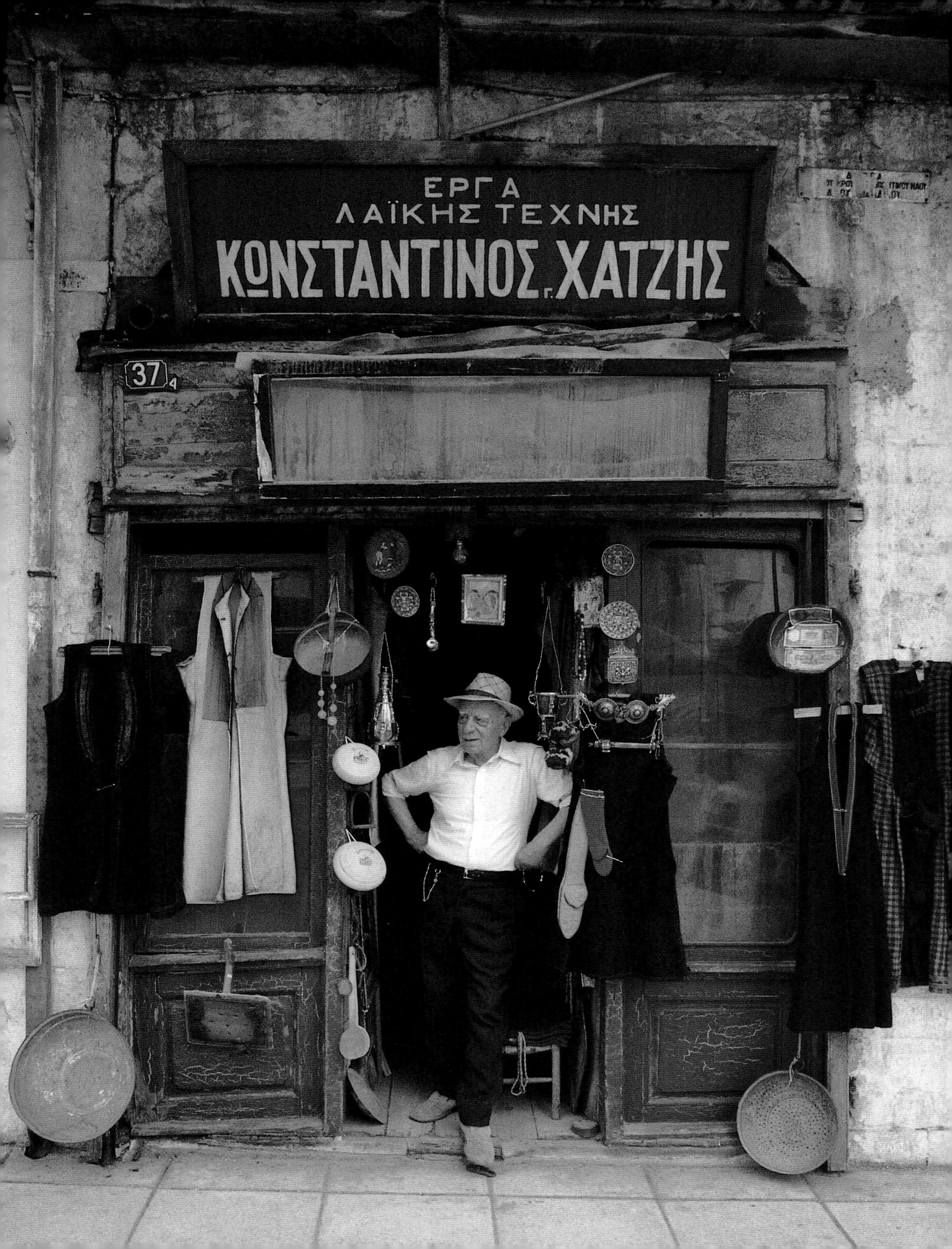
ΕΡΓΑ
ΛΑΪΚΗΣ ΤΕΧΝΗΣ
ΚΩΝΣΤΑΝΤΙΝΟΣ Γ. ΧΑΤΖΗΣ
37Α

Western Greece

Western Greece is distinguished by the celebrated Ionian coast, with its chain of islands—Corfu first among them. The waters of the Ionian Sea are deep, the deepest, in fact, of the entire Mediterranean. Sunsets upon the sea are breathtaking.

Along the coast lie the towns of Astakos, Messalonghi, Mitikas, Preveza, Parga, and Aegoumenitsa. Of these, Messalonghi and Mitikas are most famous, the former as the burial place of Lord Byron, who, fighting for Greek independence, succumbed to a fever, the latter as the locus of jet-set shenanigans, too ephemeral to describe. Except for Parga, which has a delightful beach, the coast is mainly used as the jumping-off point for other journeys, to the Ionian islands or even to Italy.

Unlike the islands and the coast (with their mild climate and harvests of tobacco and olives), the mainland is composed of the rugged country of the Epirus region, marked by mountains, rough rivers, and deep-cut valleys. Here, the Pindus mountains rise up, their sides sometimes dark-green with thick pine forests, sometimes stark with jutting rocks. The climate of the Epirus region is much colder than on the coast; in winter, the mountain passes are sometimes blocked with deep snow drifts. It is a harsh area that has been sparsely populated throughout history.

The Epirus region was noted in ancient times for launching invasions of Italy.

In addition to herding and agriculture, fishing has always played an important part in the Greek economy. This fishing boat, anchored on the Ionian coast near the town of Astakos, awaits the next job.

Here, a shop-owner of Ioannina sells antiques and other items. Ioannina is the capital of Epirus, a centre for shopping of all kinds.

Hiking is a favourite activity in the rustic Zagoria district of western Greece. Paths, such as the Kipi bridge pictured here, lead through the rough terrain, whose sights include the awesome Astraka.

Alexander the Great did so in 333 BC, as did the Epirotic ruler Pyrrhus, who followed him. However, the tide of invasion was turned in 167 BC, when the Romans landed and scourged Epirus.

High in the Pindus mountain range, about 1,000 feet above sea level, can be found the quaint village of Metsovon. The natives of Metsovon are unusually proficient in the traditional ways of Greek life, which include weaving, lace-making, and goat herding. For reasons of Greek national pride, they are subsidised by the government in creating crafts and maintaining their otherwise nomadic way of life. Thus, the village is visited by tourists and Greek natives alike, who come to enjoy the mountain air and watch the lively religious festivals, during which the villagers are dressed in native costume, which are composed of blue serge tunics, white stockings, and round toques for the men and red and black tunics with wide sleeves for women.

The native villagers of Metsovon are also unusual in that they speak a dialect that is connected to the Romance languages, and often have blue eyes. According to some sources, they are Illyrian in origin.

The Pindus mountain region is a rugged country of rich beauty. Its harsh winters, however, may fill the mountain passes with deep snow.

Tourists may see these in great numbers and think that they are nothing more than souvenir-fodder, but strings of brightly coloured beads—known as 'worry beads'—are nervously fingered throughout Greece.

In the small villages and even some cities, it is often possible to see Greeks wearing traditional costume. These vary from city to city; here in the village of Metsovon, men are wearing clothing traditional to the Pindus mountains in the Epirus region.

Here in the village of Tsepelevo, a woman makes feta cheese. Some may be surprised to learn that cheese-making still is a cottage industry; each household keeps enough for itself and sells the surplus.

81

Corfu was traditionally the entry point for invaders from western Europe. The Romans, the Normans, and the French all approached the Greek mainland through the island.

Traditional festivals are a delightful time in Metsovon. People display their folk finery on these days, such as the Festival of Saint Paraskevi during late July, and perform dances accompanied by the *bouzouki*, a stringed instrument that resembles a mandolin, and other instruments. These festivals, so important to village life, remind tourists how meaningful it is for people to come together and share common experiences.

It is in Metsovon, and other such traditional villages spread throughout the Epirus, that one may savour the type of life the Greeks lived for centuries. The Pindus mountain range has been home to several groups of nomads. They travel from field to field, and build their huts wherever their flocks come to rest. Sheep- and goatherding are especially important in the Pindus region, where the rocky soil cannot support crops. Cheese is made from the milk by the women, mainly for household use. Any surplus is quickly sold off.

Travelling down from Metsovon through the Arachthos Valley, one comes to Epirus's capital city of Ioannina, situated on Lake Ioannina (formerly Pamvotis). With a population of about 45,000, the city is the largest in the area, and has a more cosmopolitan aspect than one might expect in this sparsely populated region.

Icannina is also known as a great trading city. Many types of wares can be found here. Some are unique, traditional objects which come from artisans in the city and the surrounding villages, one of them being Metsovon.

One reason for Ioaninna's definite air of sophistication might be the spirit of Ali Pasha, the rogue Turk who governed Ioannina in the late eighteenth century. This wily ruler was renowned for turning treachery into a fine art; he betrayed a successive number of mentors and allies for an increasingly influential position. It is said that his ambition included the whole of Greece, but

This view of a sunset upon the Ionian Sea from the coastal town of Igoumenitsa, which lies on the Ionian side of Greece, puts one in the proper frame of mind for travelling through this legendary land.

*The monastery of Vlacherena covers the whole
of tiny Pontikonissi, an island just off Corfu.
The monastery dates back to the twelfth century.*

*Corfu is a modern town, with
terraced buildings and well-
paved streets. At night, the
harbour comes alive with
discos and other nightspots.*

that was not to be. He was finally betrayed into death by his own sons and in 1821, at the age of seventy-seven, executed at the citadel of Saint Panteleimon.

However devious and ambitious Ali Pasha might have been, Ioannina reached its height during his reign, becoming rich from commerce and renowned for woven goods and embroideries. Some of the more interesting buildings in the city date from the eighteenth and nineteenth centuries. One of the oldest structures, however, is the Monastery of Philanthropinos, from the thirteenth century. It contains many frescoes, all painted from that time onward.

Close to Ioannina is Dodona, which contains the ruins of many temples and what is believed to be the largest ancient theatre in Greece. The oracle of Dodona is profoundly significant, and the site has been considered sacred for almost four thousand years.

In Epirus, the spirit of independence and rebellion has always run deep. Although small and rustic, Epirus has done much to preserve the Greek way of life. The region was independent of the Byzantine Empire from the thirteenth to the fifteenth century. There was an unsuccessful revolt against the ruler Ali Pasha in 1786, and some of the leaders of the War of Independence also came from this region. During the Second World War, Epirus played a pivotal role in the Greek resistance.

Music and dancing play an important part in traditional village life. The stringed bouzouki, held by the man in the centre, produces the sound normally associated with Greek music.

Following page: These traditional costumes of the Sarakatsani in the Pindus region of western Greece indicate a large degree of Eastern influence.

This is a modern reproduction of an ecclesiastical diptych from the city of Ioannina in the Epirus region of Greece.

Dancers in traditional dress highlight the traditional festival Paraskevi, celebrated during late July in the village of Metsovon.

In the Epirus-region town of Metsovon, folkcrafts not only provoke fierce pride but are also subsidised by the government. Here, people display their traditional finery on festival days, such as this young girl at the Festival of Saint Paraskevi.

A woman stands outside a shepherd's hut in the Epirus region of Greece. Sheep and goat herding are important throughout Greece, but especially here, where the land is rocky and cannot support crops.

These stone houses in the village of Aristi are made of the rock found along the stony landscape of the Pindus mountains.

One of many frescoes to be found in the Monastery of Philanthropinos at Ioannina. Although the church itself dates from the thirteenth century, this fresco, painted by Frangos Condaris, is a sixteenth-century creation.

In Ioannina, a coppersmith's shop displays all the wares available. Traditional handicrafts, as well as imports, are a feature of the city.

This is a modern reproduction of an ecclesiastical diptych from the city of Ioannina in the Epirus region of Greece.

Dancers in traditional dress highlight the traditional festival Paraskevi, celebrated during late July in the village of Metsovon.

In the Epirus-region town of Metsovon, folkcrafts not only provoke fierce pride but are also subsidised by the government. Here, people display their traditional finery on festival days, such as this young girl at the Festival of Saint Paraskevi.

The Greek Islands

*T*here are more than two thousand islands, each beautiful in it's own way, surrounding the Greek coast. Some are green and lovely islands with sufficient water supply to support extensive agriculture, whilst others are stark and barren spots where the inhabitants must struggle to eke out a living.

THE CYCLADIC ISLANDS

The Cycladic Islands are located in the Aegean, fanning out from the coast of the Attic peninsula. They are easily reached by plane or by ferry, and might be considered the most typical of the touristic Greek islands. Their distinctive architecture, set off against sun-baked rocky hills, make them seem almost dreamlike in Mediterranean perfection.

The Cyclades are also where Neolithic sculptures, typified by wandlike bodies with the merest hint of sexual characteristics, have been found. Like Cycladic sculpture, many find these islands beautiful in their simplicity of design.

Mykonos

The Cycladic Islands are one of the most popular destinations in Greece, *the* most popular being Mykonos. Frequented by a glittery, international crowd, many Mykonos accommodations provide the amenities—such as hot water—that cannot be found in quantity on other islands.

The town of Mykonos is a beautiful place. The hot Mediterranean sun shines brightly on its attractive, whitewashed buildings, and cobblestone streets lead down to the harbour. There, it is possible to relax at a portside tavern and contemplate the Aegean and the colourful fishing boats dragged up onto the shore. The inhabitants of Mykonos adhere to a strict building code, and so all houses rise up no more than three stories, are white-washed, and rounded at their tops in a style referred to as Cycladic. The uniformity of this architecture creates a striking effect as one gazes down from one of the island's many hills, or from out at sea, or just from the harbourside. In contrast, three large windmills on a hill overlooking the harbour are painted bold colours, causing them to stand out.

At night, Mykonos's tiny central square is alive with tourists of all nations browsing through the shops (which, in this area of town, are largely given over to souvenirs) and loud music blaring from the discos. Mykonos has a reputation as a

Santorini is known for, among many other things, its churches. It has 362 of them, all of which are—like this one in the town of Oia—white with blue domes.

Donkeys laden with goods are a rather disingenuous sight on Mykonos. Almost all transportation is likely to be done on speedbikes or roaring motorised carts.

On Mykonos, the tables are lined up practically to the shoreline, while shops and restaurants overlook the water. And no wonder: the view from the harbour is one of Mediterranean serenity—blue water, with green islands looming in the distance.

real 'party town', and people are often found dressed in their seductive best, hoping to strike up new friendships. Many people say that Mykonos is over-run with tourists and is therefore less authentic than other, less visited islands, but I wonder what they really expect from a place where tourism is the principal industry. On my visit I found the small harbour town with its cosmopolitan atmosphere very pleasing.

Accommodations in Mykonos vary from tiny rooms on back streets to lovely hotels on terraced hillsides overlooking the Aegean, to luxury resorts on overcrowded beaches. Our hotel, although only a ten-minute walk from town, had that sense of serene isolation one seeks in an island visit. It was surrounded by another set of hills upon which old stone walls were built, and the moon, when it set, peeked through their lattices.

Of course, one of the main draws of Mykonos can be found in its superb beaches, which lie on the southern, mostly unpopulated side of the island. While Mykonos town also has beaches nearby, these are not as desirable, and are generally frequented by those who, having indulged all night, feel the need to stay close to home the next day. Since the town lies on the eastern coast, it is necessary to take a bus, which takes you to the end of the line at a resort area farther west. From there, one may walk over the bodies of vacationing families from all over the world—to more private and desirable beaches. Or you can take a ferry, which will bring you to Paradise (or Super Paradise) beach in no time at all. Arriving by water, one sees lonely sunbathers who prefer the solitude of the rocks rather than any beach. There are rough stone huts dotting the shore, which are said to have been built by the native shepherds.

This taverna is right on
Paradise Beach, which
is one of Mykonos' most
desirable beach spots.
Behind the taverna
is a campground where
backpackers and others
may pitch their tents.

This picturesque waterfront explains
in part why Mykonos is one of the
most visited destinations in the
Mediterranean; the other reason is its
fabulous beaches, most of which are
found on the other side of the island.

Unlike the beaches by the resorts, Mykonos' Paradise Beach seems to be only for lovers and singles who are looking for lovers. There are very few families here. The sparse crowd is made up mainly of young couples who desire privacy. One may find among the indolent sunbathers a celebrity or two, but these are generally left alone, especially if they are naked. There is a stretch of beach which is reserved for nude sunbathing, but it gets narrower and narrower every year as times change.

At Paradise Beach, the water of the Aegean is clear and quiet, and there are many small reefs harbouring interesting sealife. The beach itself is made up of small, hard, yellow pebbles, and forms a crescent surrounded by red rocks.

Super Paradise, for the most part, is for bathers of the same-sex persuasion, and by all accounts is very popular. At Super Paradise, you can take a ride on large floats shaped like a banana, pulled very close to shore by small motorboats.

Once, returning from town, I encountered a farmer who had a motorised cart filled with goats. These carts—as well as mopeds—are found everywhere on the island. Because of the reckless driving they seem to inspire, large mirrors are positioned at every turn in the road so that drivers have advance warning of oncoming traffic or pedestrians around the bend.

When returning to the mainland from Mykonos or the other islands, ferries provide a more atmospheric method of travel. From Mykonos to the port of Piraeus takes seven hours by ferry, but it provides an unforgettable experience.

This beautiful whitewashed path is typical of a Mykonos side street. Silence reigns supreme in the narrow streets during the afternoon (when everyone is inside or at the beach); only to be dispelled in the evening, as people wander to and from the town square.

A tiny line of lights along the coast is just a small indicator of Mykonos' nighttime activity. Every evening, the town of Mykonos is awash with people crowding its tiny square's tavernas, nightclubs, discos, and all-night shops.

These photographs— taken in **Mykonos** and **Santorini**, respectively— are perfect examples of what visitors to the Greek isles seek: blazing hot sun, geometrical, whitewashed buildings accentuated by bright colours.

A short glimpse of the countryside is the most that visitors—crowded on buses and headed for Mykonos' superb beaches—are likely to catch. Still, the Cycladic architecture is as striking inland as in town; and stone walls are everywhere.

Windmills upon Kato Mili hill overlook Mykonos harbour. Not only are they picturesque, but like windmills throughout Greece, they are still in use.

Here, a temple in ruins reveals a mosaic floor. Delos was sacred to the ancient Greeks since the nymph Leto fled there to bear Zeus' children, the gods Apollo and Artemis.

These enormous rampant phalluses, found on the sacred island of Delos, tell of the importance of virility to the ancient Greeks. Needless to say, they are contemplated and photographed by thousands of tourists each year.

It is not for the faint-hearted, however; the ferry engine's deafening noise—which can be heard from every part of the ship—and the rushing wind ensure that the topside ferry journey is made with few, if any words. Islands of all sizes creep by, and steep shores with red rocks, on which the occasional lighthouse is the only sign of human life. The ocean itself is alive with different colours, deep blue and purple against a crisp blue sky, or dull and sullen on a cloudy day. And on some days, sky and water marry in a pure lavender mist which has no horizon, giving you the feeling of islands and ship floating in another world.

The ferry journey can also be taken at night, and it's possible to book a cabin and get some sleep, though it's hard to say who would want to do such a thing on a clear, starry night afloat on the Aegean.

Delos

West of Mykonos, and reachable by ferry or fishing boat from there, is the island of Delos, the legendary birthplace of Apollo and Artemis. It is a barren, brown island, veined with ancient stone boundaries, venerated by the ancient Greeks as far back as 1000 BC, and now an archaeological park. There are no hotels, and only one cafeteria.

The ruins at Delos are not found in a single place, but are spread over the surface of the tiny island. Climbing its steep hills can easily tire you out, but the views of other islands in the purple Aegean Sea are breathtaking. Some of its features are the Sacred Way, which passes six stone lions—gifts of the island of Naxos—on what is called the Terrace of Lions.

The ruins range from the Naxian lions, to the enormous Apollo of Naxos (now indeterminate rubble), to partially shattered statues and temples, to lovely, well-preserved mosaic floors. Of particular interest are the potsherds that can be found

Statuary of six slender lions mark the Sacred Way, on slightly elevated ground that is also called the Terrace of Lions. As at other sacred sites, like Delphi or Olympia, it was a common practise for worshippers to commemorate their visit with gifts.

The island of Delos has been turned into an archaeological site. There, in the hot Mediterranean sun, lie the ruins of what is considered to have been the birthplace of Apollo.

Following page: Towns in the islands of the Cyclades are almost dreamlike in their Mediterranean perfection, as in the pristine whiteness of these houses and church against the clear sky and sun-baked hillside.

As in many of the islands and along the coasts of Greece, many of Santorini's indigenous population are fishermen.

everywhere, working their way out of the soil after having been buried for centuries. These are reminders that, whatever there is to be seen on Delos, there might be equal wonders not yet excavated.

Originally sacred to the ancient Greeks because the nymph Leto fled there to bear Zeus' children, the gods Apollo and Artemis, Delos' sanctity was eventually expanded to embrace many deities, both Greek and non-Greek. Statues, temples, and other memorials were raised to many gods, among them Isis and Hermes. In fact, two of the most remarkable statues, rampant phalluses mounted on pediments, are attributed to devotees of the god Hermes.

Santorini

The island of Santorini has become a very popular tourist destination in recent years. Although the population of its chief city, Thera, is no more than two thousand in the off-season, the town and its outskirts spill over during the summer. The tourists come to bask on the island's unusual black-sand beaches (made of crumbled volcanic rock), and to delight in the spectacular Mediterranean sunsets.

The Cycladic Islands are often visited by white pelicans. These birds—almost the size of a person—are so coveted as 'mascots' that when they die or otherwise depart, some islands go out of their way to import them.

Like many island towns in the Cyclades group, Thera is a picturesque city built into the island's steep slopes. Its houses are typically whitewashed Venetian-Cycladic architecture, and there are literally hundreds of domed churches. It is a heady feeling to be standing up above the city of Thera and gaze down at the Aegean below, and out at nearby islands on the horizon. The steps are built zig-zag into the steep rock, and make for a bracing climb.

Santorini, a crescent-shaped island, is actually the remains of an ancient volcano, which exploded between 1600-1450 BC, sinking half the island. This half remains 1,200 feet (366 metres) underwater

The off-season population of Santorini is quite small, with no more than an estimated fifteen hundred yearlong residents in the town of Thera. This number balloons enormously during the season, when visitors come, among other things, to enjoy the sunsets.

Naxos was famous in the ancient world for its marble, some of which can be found on Delos in the form of six remarkable lion sculptures. Nowadays, it is a favourite destination for tourists.

A characteristic of the Greeks that is often commented upon is their garrulity. All over the country, including this storefront in the Cyclades, people gather to talk.

Santorini's beautiful churches were, by some accounts, built as a sort of 'tax dodge'. Land on which a church was built could not be taxed by the Ottoman tax collectors.

to this day. The island's volcanic heritage can be discerned in the cliffs—the sides of the caldera—from which stream red and white minerals into the Aegean, and Santorini's unusual beaches, which are black with ash. But the island is relatively stable now. The most recent earthquake was nearly thirty-five years ago.

Santorini is also renowned for the excavations of a Bronze Age settlement near Thera, at Akrotiri. Its discovery predates Hellenic civilisation and is contemporaneous with the Minoan civilisation of Crete. In fact, some speculate that tidal waves created by the Santorini eruption were responsible for the destruction of Cretan civilisation, and others believe that Santorini, also known as *Calliste*, or Most Beautiful, in ancient times, was none other than Atlantis. It is possible to view the frescoes, temple foundations, and other recovered artifacts and enjoy one's own speculations.

Naxos

The town of Apirathos on the island of Naxos was once the playground of wealthy Greeks, and retains much of its quaintness. Local residents may pull picturesque donkey carts along its narrow streets, amidst the numerous specimens of eighteenth- and nineteenth-century architecture.

Naxos was famous in the ancient world for its marble, some of which can be found on Delos in the form of six remarkable lion sculptures. Nowadays, it is a favourite destination for tourists from all over the world.

Naxos boasts tiny villages like Ano Sangri, where the villagers still perform traditional activities—such as spinning and cheese-making—in the ancestral way.

The town of Apirathos on Naxos was once the abode of the wealthy. It is still beautiful, and retains many specimens of eighteenth- and nineteenth-century architecture along quaint, narrow streets. streets.

Spinning is still done by hand throughout Greece, as this old woman in the tiny village of Ano Sangri on the island of Naxos demonstrates.

Pictured is the temple of Aphaia, one of the best-preserved examples of Archaic architecture left. The island of Aegina is part of the Saronic Gulf chain, and lies between mainland Greece and the Pelopponesos.

Milos

The little island of Milos, whose name means 'quince' or 'apple', has had a luckless history. It was first distinguished by the terrible massacre and enslavement of its people by the Athenians in the fifth century BC, an act which is thought to have provoked the historian Thucydides into picking up his pen. More recently, it has been known as the site of the discovery of the Venus de Milo in 1820, which was subsequently trundled off to the Louvre.

Today, it is a quiet little island, which subsists by growing crops of the traditional Mediterranean trio of grain, grapes, and olives.

In Passing

Sifnos is a beautiful island, but lacks the steady supply of water needed to make it a top tourist destination, a fate it shares with Ios. Also beautiful is the island of Siros; the chief town, Ermoupoli, is a glory of neoclassical architecture.

The village of Thera on Santorini is achingly stark against the blue Mediterranean sky. The steps leading through the village are built zig-zag fashion into the steep rock, and make for a bracing climb.

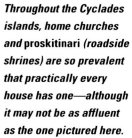

Throughout the Cyclades islands, home churches and proskitinari *(roadside shrines) are so prevalent that practically every house has one—although it may not be as affluent as the one pictured here.*

On the Cycladic island of Sifnos, a whitewashed path leads from the coast to the church. Like Ios, Sifnos does not have a large water supply, which makes it awkward for tourism.

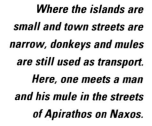

Where the islands are small and town streets are narrow, donkeys and mules are still used as transport. Here, one meets a man and his mule in the streets of Apirathos on Naxos.

THE DODECANESE ISLANDS

This group of islands in the southeastern Aegean is a popular tourist destination and during the Renaissance was a stronghold of the Venetians and Genoese in the eastern Mediterranean. From 1923 to 1947, the islands were an Italian possession, restored to Greece after the defeat of the Axis in World War II. The name, Dodecanese, refers to the twelve principal islands of the archipelago.

Rhodes

Of the islands of the Dodecanese, Rhodes is the first and foremost, both in size and in history. Rhodes was originally colonised in 1000 BC by Dorians from the Peloponnesian peninsula, who established the cities of Ialysos, Lindos, and Camiros. The cities soon prospered, and settlers agreed to form a fourth town in the late fifth century BC. This was the city of Rhodes, and it soon became and remained a prosperous trading city.

In antiquity, Rhodes was famous for the enormous bronze statue set in its harbour (now known as Mandraki), which was made to commemorate the Rhodian victory over Demetrios of Syria around 305 BC. Twelve years in the making, it became the one of Seven Wonders of the World, only to collapse in an earthquake in 225 BC. As the legends tell it, the Rhodians were forbidden by the Delphic Oracle to raise the Colossus again, and it was left lying in pieces around the harbour, mouldering in the sun, until it was sold as scrap-metal. The harbour now has columns, set with the city's symbols of stag and doe, which commemorate the place where the Colossus reputedly once stood.

In Greece's long history of siege and occupation, Rhodes is particularly famous for its conquest by the Crusaders in the fourteenth century. Repelled by the Saracens (who held the Holy Land) the Crusaders fell back and instead claimed Rhodes. The Hospitallers built this fortress, called the Palace of the Grand Masters, and held it until the sixteenth century.

The town of Lindos has been inhabited since Dorian times. The ancient ruins of the propylaea of the Sanctuary of Athena were restored by the Italians (who occupied the island until 1947) to show off the impressive proportions of the building, as well as the site.

Following page: The island of Rhodes is resplendent with the past, as this photograph taken from the Mandraki Harbour demonstrates. In the foreground stands the medieval watchtower, and in the distance a minaret which dates from the Turkish occupation.

Among the islands of Greece, Rhodes has a particularly military atmosphere. It was conquered in turn by the Romans, the Crusaders, the Venetians, and the Turks—all of whom built fortresses. Here above the town of Lindos is its ancient Acropolis, with the Sanctuary of Athena visible amid medieval foundations.

Rhodes' next notable episode occurred in the fourteenth century. The Maltese Knights of Saint John, driven from the Holy Land, sought refuge at Rhodes. Rhodes was then a territory belonging to the Byzantine Empire, but the Knights seized the island for their own, with the blessing of the Roman Catholic Church. The Knights' ownership included all of the windmills on the island, to each of which they gave the name of a saint.

The Knights built many fortresses on Rhodes, including the Palace of the Grand Masters. They were an international order, and the fortress walls were defended in sections by 'tongues'—companies of men divided into groups according to their native languages. The tongues set up their own residences, called inns, in what is now the Street of the Knights, and these may be seen today in the Old Town. Other mementoes of the Knights include the fortress called the Hospital, as well as the Church of the Knights at Ialysos, with a huge

Maltese cross carved into the side of the bell tower.

In the sixteenth century, the Turks drove the Knights out of Rhodes, and the Sultan Suleiman built a large mosque directly adjacent from the hospital. The Turks in turn lost Rhodes to the Italians during the Italo-Turkish Conflict which succeeded the War of Independence, and the island did not return to the Greek national fold until 1947, after the Second World War.

Rhodes is a partly green island with a sufficient water supply for agriculture; crops of olives, wine, fruit, grain, and cotton are raised and exported from its fertile interior. As far as the tourism trade along the coast, it is just as sunny as any of the Cyclades, and so enjoys good business.

The town of Lindos, one of the oldest settlements on the island, is now a thriving tourist town, with a much-visited beach. Visitors tanning themselves on the beach can look up and behold the ruins of the old Acropolis; the propylaea of the sanctuary of Athena is ringed by the ruins of medieval fortifications.

Pictured here at Rhodes are windmills. An invention of the Middle Ages, windmills continue to serve Greece; on Rhodes, they were once owned by the Church, which gave them the names of the saints.

Simi, with its whitewashed, square-cut houses set against sun-baked hills, looks like it might be from another century.

Lindos, a town on the island of Rhodes, has many characteristics of Greek Mediterranean architecture, such as these domed, whitewashed houses and red-tiled roofs.

Kos

In antiquity, Kos was a centre of the cult of Aesclapios; in fact, the great Hippocrates (460 BC), considered the Father of Modern Medicine, hailed from here. Like Rhodes, Kos was also seized by the Knights of Saint John, who built substantial fortifications around its harbour.

Today, it has a robust tourist industry, and though considerably smaller, is the most popular Dodecanese island after Rhodes. Part of its charm is based on its considerable prettiness, which is enhanced by the ruins of Roman, Crusader, and Turkish occupation, as well as the attraction of good beaches. The island also features cave dwellings with ancient rock carvings, as well as thermal springs in its eastern section.

Patmos

Patmos is blessed in Christian memory as the place of exile for Saint John of the Cross, author of the Biblical Book of the Revelation, in AD 96. The Monastery of Saint John, consecrated to his memory, is on the island, and celebrated its nine hundredth anniversary in 1988.

The Dodecanese island of Rhodes is considered a 'green' island, less sun-baked than, say, those of the Cycladic chain. For this reason, it is a very popular vacation spot for Greek nationals. Still, it also has what the tourists crave: beaches and some small, beautiful ports.

Though Patmos has a steady tourist trade, it is also an island of small villages and farms. Here the villagers gather to celebrate the religious holidays, which are important to them, especially Easter, when the town of Patmos reenacts the story of the Last Supper.

The island is completely cultivated in the method used all over mountainous Greece, namely terrace farming. Its rocky slopes are braced by walls, which keep the topsoil from eroding and form pocket-size fields suitable for cultivation.

In Passing

Other islands of the Dodecanese include Simi, a pretty island with a nineteenth-century harbour; Kalymnos, known for its sponge-fishing industry; Karpathos, where the women's traditional costume is of dark wool shot with vibrant embroidery and includes the *kolaina*, a necklace made of coins; and quiet Leros, with its yacht station and airfield.

THE AEGEAN ISLANDS

The Aegean Islands include Chios, Lesbos, Limenas, Limnos, Mirina, Samos, Samothraki, Skala Prinos, and Thassos; they lie just off the western coast of Turkey. Some romantics might claim that the soul of Greece first breathed upon the Aegean Islands, for it was on the isle of Chios that Homer first began to sing of the Trojan War, and on Lesbos that the soft-spoken lyric poetry of Sappho and Alcaeus was first heard.

Fishing boats with their brightly coloured sails
furled glide in the calm waters of the harbour at
Kos. The scene—sleepy and serene—belies the
fact that Kos has become a key tourist destination.

Rice flies through the air to commemorate this Greek Orthodox wedding, performed on the island of Kos. In Greece, about ninety-seven percent of the population follows the Greek Orthodox religion.

On the island of Patmos, villagers break into folk dancing at the mayor's party. They are celebrating Easter.

Patmos has a sacred memory for Christians everywhere: In AD 96, it was a place of exile for St John. Here, Orthodox priests preside at a Maundy Thursday celebration prior to Easter.

Terraced farming, which prevents the topsoil from eroding, is typical of Greece, where three-quarters of the country is mountainous and the islands rise swiftly from the sea. These terraced fields are on the island of Patmos.

At the Mandraki Harbour entrance in the city of Rhodes, it's easy to believe that the past can come alive. These pedestals, graced with the symbols of Rhodes, mark where the legs of the famous Colossus were supposed to have stood.

On Rhodes, a medieval watchtower built by Crusaders serves as a backdrop for the quaint harbour square with its fountain and contemporary cafes.

Samos

The island of Samos was once wealthy and drew the creme of Classical Greek intelligentsia—Pythagoras and Aesop among them—to its shores. This happy situation soon deteriorated; probably Samos's grain shortages in the third century BC contributed to the matter. The current indigenous population is descended from seventeenth-century settlers, whom the local Turkish government sent to recolonise the island after it had been savaged by pirates.

The charming town of Pythagorion, named after Pythagoras, is made up for the most part of houses which are no more than two stories tall. Fishing is still a big industry in Samos, as it is in much of Greece.

Samos's antique attractions include the Temple of Hera, once the largest temple in the ancient world, of which only one pillar now remains, and the Eupalinus Tunnel, a sixth-century BC aqueduct which piped mountain water to the coastal city. The island is now a resort for those seeking a more low-key experience than that offered by the Dodecanese or Cyclades, and the pebbly grey beaches have proved quite popular.

Chios

Chios has seen many disasters, natural and man-made, since the time of Homer in 850 BC. For more

than one hundred years, the land has been ravaged by earthquakes and forest fires. Today's Chios little resembles the land that Homer—or indeed anyone prior to 1888—knew. There are a few fortunate exceptions, including the medieval towns of Pirgi and Mesta.

Chios derives its income less from tourism than from shipbuilding and the local chewing gum industry, but many visitors do come to walk Emborios's black stone beaches, located in the western part of the island. Chios has other, more unusual attractions, one of which is the town of Pirgi, where the exteriors of buildings are composed of *xysta*, in which geometrical designs are applied onto buildings by alternating grey and white layers of plaster, then scraping away the top layer to reveal the one below.

Samothraki

Samothraki is famous for its Winged Victory sculpture, which now—like other priceless examples of antiquity—resides in the Louvre. It is an island that, while not of great interest to tourists, is fascinating to archaeologists for the mysteries that date back to Phoenician times. Excavations, ongoing since 1938, have uncovered the foundations of a great religious complex.

The tiny but beautiful village of Molyvos belies the fact that Lesbos is one of the most populated islands in Greece. On the outskirts of Molyvos there is a Genoese fortress which dates from the Middle Ages.

Lesbos

Lesbos is one of the most populous islands in Greece. Together with Chios and other Aegean islands, Lesbos was once owned by the Genoese in the thirteenth century—trifles handed over by the Byzantine Empire for assistance rendered against the Venetians. Thus, it is possible to see a fourteenth-century Genoese fortress on the outskirts of the town of Molyvos, as well as the fortress of Gatilusi in the town of Mytilini. The island itself was once called Mytilini. It is much better known, of course, under its original name of Lesbos, which has entered into Western culture as the root word of lesbianism, a common term for sexual love between women. Indeed, the ancient Greeks had a verb, *lesbiadzou*, which meant, more or less, certain scandalous practices. Lesbos was the birthplace of lyric poetry, whose beautiful rhythms were borrowed by the Attic tragedians to form the chorus.

In Passing

Tucked in close to the Thracian coast, Thasos has a Hellenic amphitheatre where ancient plays are performed during festivals and is famous for its pine-tree honey, supposedly the best in Greece. To its south, Limnos is known for its first-class resort, Akti Myrina, and a Venetian fortress which is, Parthenon-style, bombarded with coloured lights at night.

At Mytilini on the island of Lesbos, the ruins of the medieval fortress of the Gatilusi—the Genoese family to whom the island belonged in the late fourteenth century—can be found.

Agios Nikolaos, on the island of Crete, takes its name from a nearby church of the Byzantine period. The serene harbour, seen here, was actually a lake until the late nineteenth century, when a canal was dug to connect it to the sea.

CRETE

Crete, the sunny island some 96 kilometres (60 miles) south of the Cycladic isle of Santorini, stands at the forefront of Western civilisation. Sites of human habitation dating back to Neolithic times can be found, but the excavations at Phaistos and Knossos, begun in the nineteenth century, tell of another Crete: the Bronze Age dominion of the Sea Kings, whose trade and conquests spread throughout the Mediterranean thousands of years before the dawn of Hellenic culture—indeed, long before the Trojan War.

Sir Arthur Evans, the primary excavator of Knossos, had reconstructed parts of the palace, such as the entrance hall, the throne of the kings, and others by the turn of the century. Evans was both the blessing and the curse of archaeology: His vision and enthusiasm spurred interest in the discoveries at Crete throughout Europe, but he also made dreadful, amateurish mistakes, such as leaving newly discovered sherds of writing exposed to the elements and thereby losing a priceless find.

Following page: This fortress, overlooking the town of Rethymnon in Crete, was built by the Venetians in 1574. The island of Crete, with its key position in respect to Europe, Asia Minor, and Africa, has been contested right up until this century.

135

There has been some reconstruction at the Palace at Knossos, in order to give some idea what the palace must have looked like in its heyday. Unlike so much of the whitewashed architecture typical of the rest of Greece, these restored rooms shine with vibrant colour. The typically top-heavy columns of Minoan design are painted black and burnt sienna and a wall and doorway are frescoed in undulating Minoan patterns.

Some of the brilliant frescoes, the originals of which have been removed to the archaeological museum at Iraklio (Candia), are merely abstract patterns, while others portray bulls and human figures. Everyone is familiar with the story of King Minos, who had an intricate labyrinth constructed by the legendary inventor Daedelus to imprison the half-man, half-bull Minotaur. Certainly the roots of the myth are present at Knossos: the palace corridors can be considered labyrinthine, and bulls, judging by the colourful frescoes that have survived, were undoubtedly sacred to the ancient Minoans.

Ancient Cretan culture was said to have been fatally stricken by the huge tidal waves created by the eruption of Santorini's volcano in 1450 BC, although the cities of Phaistos and Knossos were far inland enough to be spared. Nonetheless, Minoan civilisation seems to have come to an end about that time.

Modern-day Crete is still bustling with archaeological excavations which are open to public view. These include the Hagia Triada, whose ruins appear tranquil amid the grass-grown landscape; Malia, a smaller, less-splendid palace ruin; and Gournia, a post-Minoan settlement on the northern coast of the island.

Today, Crete is still a memorable island. Like much of Greece, its economy is mainly agricultural, relying on the ancient Mediterranean triangle of cereals, olives, and vineyards—especially vineyards. The Cretan landscape is alive with groves of olives and fruit, and grape vines. Other industries include fishing and goatherding—the latter provides islanders with wool, meat, and cheese.

Crete also has ruins that attest to the fight for its possession and occupation by others. There is a fortress, overlooking the town of Rethymnon, built by the Venetians in 1574. The sixteenth-century Venetian fortezza is easily recognised by its prominent dome.

Rethymnon is located on the northern coast of Crete, where the island's maritime industry has traditionally been strongest. The well-kept lighthouse and seawall attest to the continued importance of sea trade.

Windmills, that revolutionary invention of the Middle Ages, have not lost their importance on Crete. At Lasithi to the west, they dominate so much of the landscape that it is called the Valley of the Windmills.

The principal city of Crete is Candia, also known as Herakleion or Iraklio, whose whitewashed buildings cluster along the coast and deeper inland. Among these are the typical domed Greek churches with roofs that are vibrantly coloured. One may walk along the seawall that projects into the harbour and also serves to berth fishing boats and other small craft.

Inland, Mount Ida looms, 23 miles (37 kilometres) from top to sea level. At 2,456 metres high (almost 8,000 feet) Mount Ida is said to have been the birthplace of Zeus, and it certainly looks the part. You can hike up to the Idean Cave, supposedly the actual site of Zeus' birth, high on the slopes. Its snow-covered sides are some wreathed in mist. Approach to the mountain is difficult, marked in many places by pitted gullies and a stark landscape.

The people of Crete long held out against the invading Turks, succumbing only in the seventeenth century. Thanks to the brief Turkish influence, short, gathered trousers, sashes, and boots have become part of native Cretan dress.

Crete also has a famous monastery—the monastery of Arkadi—but unlike those at Mount Athos and the Meteora (as well as lesser monasteries throughout Greece), the

Minoan civilisation was at its height around 1450 BC, when it inexplicably collapsed. Many believe that a tsunami—a giant tidal wave—created by a volcanic eruption on Thera (now Santorini) destroyed the ancient Cretan cities, throwing the civilisation into turmoil.

Myrtos Beach, a narrow spit of sand along the coast of the Ionian island of Cephalonia, is considered by some to be one of the best—if somewhat inaccessible—beaches in Greece.

Unlike the famous monasteries of Mount Athos and the Meteora (as well as lesser monasteries throughout Greece), the monastery of Arkadi on Crete was built in the sixteenth century by the Venetians; its monks were Roman Catholic rather than Greek Orthodox. In 1866, the Abbot chose to explode the monastery's supply of gun powder rather than surrender to the besieging Turks.

sixteenth-century monastery was established by the Venetians, therefore its monks were Roman Catholic rather than Greek Orthodox. In 1866, the Abbot chose to explode the monastery's supply of gunpowder rather than surrender to the besieging Turks.

Nowadays, Crete is famous for its splendid beaches and as the home of author Nikos Kazantzakis, whose book *Zorba the Greek*, established the ebullient Greek character in modern literature and film, and whose controversial *The Last Temptation of Christ* was made into a film, directed by Martin Scorsese.

THE IONIAN ISLANDS

The Ionian Islands, which include Corfu, Antipaxos, Laphkada, Cephalonia, and Ithaca, combine the mystique of Homeric legend with the insistent march of Western history. They are set along the northwestern coast of Greece in the Ionian Sea, where the Mediterranean runs deepest.

Corfu

In his book *Prospero's Cell*, Lawrence Durrell rhapsodised about life in the Ionian Islands in the 1930s. He portrayed his sojourn here as an idyllic life of philosophising with the local men of letters, fishing for one's dinner, and waiting for the supply ship to arrive. Even now, developed as it is for the tourist trade, the town of Corfu is still lovely, with terraced buildings and well-paved streets. Its nightlife may be boisterous, with discos and other night spots lining the harbour, but that is not unusual in the Greek islands.

The island of Corfu was originally settled in the eighth century BC by the Dorians, who expanded their colonies throughout the Mediterranean from their base in the Peloponnisos. The island succumbed peacefully to the Romans in the first century AD, and as a Roman colony probably had the longest respite from war that it would have until the present day.

For Corfu was the point of entry to Greece for invaders from western Europe. It was repeatedly stormed by invaders, including barbarians, Sicilians, Venetians, the Turks, and the French. One final indignity came during the Second World War, when the Italians used the town for target practise.

Today, Corfu is lively with the trade of both tourists—who enjoy the coast towns and sunny beaches—and Greek nationals, who favour the verdant interior. Testaments to the island's various occupations abound, especially in the old town, where the vestiges of old fortresses can still be seen.

Also to be found are solemn olive groves. The olive has played an important part in Corfu's agriculture since ancient times. In fact, some trees of its groves look like they might have greeted Odysseus on his arrival.

Corfu's Paleo Kastritsa monastery—with its whitewashed walls and belfry—is a favourite destination of visitors, as is Lake Korisson to the west and the beautiful beaches on the southern coast.

Off the coast of Corfu is the islet of Pontikonissi (also called Mouse Island). Legend says it was originally the ship which carried Odysseus, and was turned to stone by the sea god Poseidon. Now, the monastery of Vlacherena, dating back to the twelfth century, covers the whole of tiny Pontikonissi.

Ithaca

Craggy Ithaca, off the east coast of the much larger island of Cephalonia, was the legendary home of Odysseus, the wily king who reluctantly followed Agamemnon to the siege of Troy, and the hero of the *Odyssey*, whose homecoming (twenty years in the making) spelled death for his wife's undesirable suitors. Odysseus was actually considered a demigod in some precincts of Greece, so places associated with him—such as the Arethousa spring and Grotto of the Nymphs—have a certain power.

Ithaca, with its quiet fishing villages and rugged interior, remains relatively untouched by Greece's tourist boom, although a journey to Odysseus's isle would not be wasted.

In Passing

Cephalonia is a charming place of beautiful sand beaches and a tiny harbour accessible only through a constricted channel. The island of Laphkada to the north is separated from the mainland of Greece by an extremely narrow channel only 37 metres (120 feet) in width. This channel is now crossed by a broad causeway.

Crete is the largest island in Greece and, as evidenced by this picture, enjoys a great popularity among summer visitors.

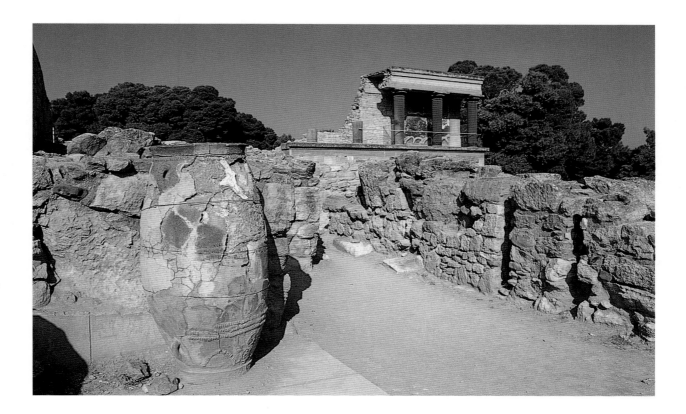

The blood-red columns and fresco in the distance set off the Minoan palace near the present-day city of Iraklion. The palace was built between 1900-1540 BC. The site was controversially renovated by its discoverer, Sir Arthur Evans.

Afterword

Today, as Greece continues to grow into the twentieth century, it is also doing something which not many nations can boast of: gaining in land mass without going to war. Recent measurements taken from satellite pictures confirm that Greece is expanding.

While about half of Greece's population can be found outside the cities, the country itself is becoming increasingly urban, and a number of people are abandoning the islands and the countryside for the cities every year.

Greece is now a bustling member of the European Community, and Athens is a sophisticated capital. In preparation for European unification, Greece has sought to impose the Western working hours of nine to five, as opposed to the Mediterranean norm of a long siesta following lunch, then work from four until eight. This change has had the added advantage of eliminating the four rush hours which used to plague

Rethymnon is located on the northern coast of Crete,
where the island's maritime industry has traditionally
been strongest. This well-kept lighthouse and seawall
attest to the continued importance of sea trade.

the streets of Athens.

Greece's politics remain the most exciting in Europe. The military regime of 1967-1974, during which the Greek constitution was suspended and the country repressed by the colonels' ultra-rightist administration, gave way to a new constitution in 1974. Instead of calming down, Greece has seen elections held almost on a monthly basis, prime ministers who have thrown out their entire cabinets, and kings waiting in the wings to see if their time has come. Attempts have been made, however, to reconcile Greece and Turkey, those ancient enemies. 'The spirit of Davos', which refers to a meeting of Papandreou and the Turkish Prime Minister Turgut Ozal in 1988, has led to a relaxation of enmity between the two nations.

Thus, while tourists continue to seek the timelessness of Greece, the country itself is keeping in step with the rest of the European community, making its way into the twenty-first century.

High above the town of Rethymnon in Crete, the dome of the sixteenth-century Venetian fortezza can be seen as the sun sets.

INDEX